The Campion Company Story

by

Dave Crofts

Copyright © 2016 Dave Crofts

All rights reserved, including the right to reproduce this book, or portions thereof in any form. No part of this text may be reproduced, transmitted, downloaded, decompiled, reverse engineered, or stored, in any form or introduced into any information storage and retrieval system, in any form or by any means, whether electronic or mechanical without the express written permission of the author.

ISBN: 978-1-326-74957-6

PublishNation
www.publishnation.co.uk

CAMPION CONTENTS

Front Cover features inside the Campion factory, Robin Hood St, Nottingham. Dated 1904.

The Authors restored 1921 4HP.	Page 1
INTRODUCTION	Page 2-4
TEXTILES	Pages 5-7
FACTORIES	Pages 8-14
BICYCLES	Pages 15-38
MOTORCYCLES	Pages 39-61
SIDECARS	Pages 62-68
CARS	Pages 69-72
COMPETITION	Pages 73-83
WARTIME	Pages 84-95
ASSOCIATIONS	Pages 96-103
INNOVATION	Pages 104-111
HENRY CURRY	Pages 112-114
FINALLY	Page 115
BIBLIOGRAPHY	Page 116
PICTURE CREDITS	Page 117
ACKNOWLEDGEMENTS	Page 118
Photograph of New Gerrard, outside 13 Wheeler Gate, Nottingham, 1926.	Page 119

CAMPION INTRODUCTION

In the 1970's I worked as Saturday lad at Horne's, a gentleman's outfitters, situated on the corner of Long Row and Clumber St, Nottingham. Just a few doors up was the White Lion Public House, where in 1908, the Nottingham Motorcycle Club met for the first time. Directly opposite Horne's, was the first Boots Chemist, which stood proudly amongst the other shops, embellished by its curved glass frontage. Going up from this junction was Pelham St, that lead to the famous Lace Market, which was not a market as such, but a maze of alley ways and industrial revolution buildings that in its day was the busiest part of Nottingham, and Nottingham was a very busy City. Full of people, and full of noise. The clattering of lace machines, frame makers and blacksmiths. Here in the centre of the City.

Everything entered the Lace market via Woolpack Lane. Not by lorries and vans hindered by restricted access, or met with no parking signs, one way streets, double yellow lines, and pedestrianised areas, but by men with horses, carts, barrows, and lots of them. Come 1900 this began to change with the first motorized goods vehicles, forecars and motorcycles.

With all the melee of people in this area, refreshment was a necessity, so public houses were littered everywhere. Indeed, the public house was where people of all classes met, drank, ate, kept warm, and did most of their business deals. It is so sad that these places have gone?

You have to image the stench, overcrowding, and general chaos of activity. Despite this the average person was relatively happy. They had bread on the table, they could pay the rent in the new housing that were being built. They could go to the pub, and could afford arguably, a family and a pint. Jobs were becoming a plenty, although health and safety was, still in its early formation. The Lace Market boasted four steam-powered engines in 1860, driving lace and hosiery machinery in the mills. More were added. Water was plentiful by way of the River Leen. Coal for the steam engines came from the County, as did food and so did some of the beer. In all it was a better life than before, but life was changing rapidly with technology and entrepreneurs.

Competition was fierce, but strangely enough in those days, people pulled together in industry. More often than not, they helped each other with engineering problems, unlike now. Jealously guarded patents were not that regular. Nottingham saw for its one and only time, an expanse of its City Industrial areas that was black, dirty, noisy, and very crowded but surprising with skilled labour, and above all, they were making money.

A black industrial plague hung over the City, reaching overnight into the outer areas of the City, with its fingers lingering over the Canal and the River Trent. So much was happening so soon. It is here on Woolpack Lane that a William Campion began our story, in his own mill, his own factory, making frames and lockstitch machinery for the other factories, that were for sale not just in Nottingham, but through agents in London.

It is important to realize that the motorcycle was a slow evolution from the bicycle, which in turn evolved from everyday machinery. To paint the picture correctly I have to go back, and reflect on the Campion family and their story. Do you want to see one of my average watercolor paintings or a real Rembrandt? Obvious answer to that, and I hope that's what you will see, feel, and smell here. The emphasis on this era is so important to portray in Nottingham during our story. Especially if you consider the other famous names associated with Nottingham.

It is also important that Nottingham should remember the sheer brilliance not just of one person, but a whole family of engineers that contributed greatly to Nottingham's economy and success, that I feel has been sadly overlooked.

I must apologize for being opinionated on this subject, but hopefully so shall you once you have read the material gathered here that has not been seen before. I have restored many bikes and cars over the years, having both ridden and shown them at many shows, as well as judging concours both here and abroad. I have fallen from a few to?

This is my first Campion Motorcycle, and unless I find another, probably the last. She came as a wreck, but don't they all? All wrecks are restorable. No swapping bits from other bikes on this baby, you've have to make them kid!!!! Loads of fun, and that I have had. This initially inspired the Campion Story.

I looked at the usual internet searches that tended to copy each other, and I thought there's more to this than meets the eye. Three years later, two computers, piles of scraps of paper with notes and phone numbers thereon, I have indeed found a great deal of information.

All is documented. It is no good just sitting here, gathering dust so suitably inspired I began to put it all together for you to read.

Even if you are not a cyclist, biker, or general motor head, there is an abundance of local history, names and facts to explore. It includes locations in Nottingham, textiles, and the impact of the Great War on industry and Nottingham people. It is all collated and put together, but that does not mean its finished? Out there, are more of you who have a picture, a memory, and a story to tell? Let me know, and let's nail it down for volume 2.

And so it begins. I hope you also will become a **CAMPIONITE?**

Here we have the only known photograph of William Campion. Taken 1880 by Mr E. Steal, with credit to Mr H. Holdsworth, and gratitude to Picture the Past for allowing this to be used with numerous other photos in the book. His Son Edwin looked remarkably like him and so did George Campion.

CAMPION TEXTILES

Those of you that have studied genealogy would have hours of entertainment over the Campion family. Regarding this chapter, I have kept it simple, and not talked of other family members that shadow the main characters who contributed to the Campion story. With one exception, William Campion. As the story goes, William Campion came from Leicester to Nottingham in the 1840`s. He was a blacksmith and frame maker that had a partnership with a Mr Johnson in the lace market. There were a number of patents and activity with textile machinery up to 1860 when the partnership is said to have been dissolved. At this point another William Campion, either nephew or cousin became involved with patents. He is named as successor to the previous William so you have to be careful to identify who was where and when? To make matters more confusing, a little later there are also two William Campion`s residing on Blue Bell Hill in Nottingham, and both are recorded as bicycle makers? My thanks again to Brian Binns for sorting this, as at times it really clouded my vision and objective.

1859. William Campion was in partnership with Henry Johnson at the Hoyles Factory, Woolpack Lane, Nottingham. Here they manufacture machinery and had a working mill. In this year there was the first patent 876 to do with machinery.

1860. William Campion and William Campion (junior) had their first patent 1569 regarding sewing machines.

1862. William Campion has his own business established as a sewing machine maker on Aberdeen Street. This is located just around the corner from the Liverpool St.

1864. Newton Wilson begins to manufacture sewing machines at the Hoyles Factory, with Johnson still in partnership with William Campion. It was stated the partnership was over but obviously not? The machines made here were initially copies of Singers and Howe, (American Companies) which later ended in court cases with the respective companies. Court cases were draining Newton Wilson financially, and in 1866 he was declared bankrupt. This did not stop him in other pursuits discussed in the Bicycle Chapter, but the timing of this is crucial. William Campion continued producing his own sewing machines. I believe there are only three left in existence, and are very collectable not only for their scarcity but quality.

1870. Patent 3190 of 1867 regarding machines were awarded to William Campion of Nottingham.

1870. The Jenny Lind machine was registered. Also produced were the Lady and Progress, which were small and portable. Again these are very collectable.

1873. William Campion and William Campion, one of Nottingham, the other being from Snienton (mechanic) took out an American patent number US139114A to do with improving knitting machines by being able to change a machine to do narrow work.

1875. The business was sold to Augustine Hind, and closed the following year.

1877. Hind took William Campion to court over the reliability and performance of the Machines. There was a long court case but Hind did not win.

> **VIEW TUESDAY NEXT. SALE WEDNESDAY, 11 A.M.**
> **TO HOSIERY MANUFACTURERS, MACHINE BUILDERS, AND OTHERS.**
> TWENTY-SEVEN CAMPION'S PATENT ROTARY MACHINES, namely, Shirt Body, Sleeving, Hose, Legging, Footing and Heeling Frames; also one Rib-top Frame, and the PLANT for the MANUFACTURE of SEWING MACHINES, recently used by Mr. William Campion. The whole, as now standing in Room No. 1, Windley's Factory, Robin Hood-street, will be SOLD by AUCTION, by Mr. WHITEHEAD, on Wednesday, December 11, 1878, at Eleven o'clock. On view the two days previously from Ten to Four. Catalogues on application at the Mart, Milton-street. 3357

This is an important advert from 1878, showing the location as Robin Hood St. Thanks to BNA.

William cleared his entire stock of machinery, which was more considerable than shown above. This included silk spinning machinery and stated that he was now retiring from the textile trade. He took on The Sir Colin Campbell public house at 11 Robin Hood Street, which remained in the family for twenty years, but did he finish entirely, or was it just a ploy to elude Hind in Court? Textile manufacture did continue, and further patents were to follow.

1879. An English patent by William Campion, also in America by 1881, US201881. An automatic Jacquard-knitting machine relating to close or open fabrics.

1888. William Campion and H.B. Payne took out an American patent US 395075 to do with machines for lacing jacquard cards.

1889. William Campion and H.B. Payne took out a patent in America US397140A, to do with warp knitting machines. Originally filed in 1886.

1892. Interestingly William Campion of Brooklyn, New York, took out the patent regarding warp-knitting machines. It is impossible to decide which of the Williams were responsible, but at least their efforts are finally recorded. The American patents were taken out in New York and Washington. The plans of these machines are most intriguing with wonderful attention to detail. The younger William Campion is more likely to be our man with these American connections, simply due to age. William`s son Edwin, had taken on the management of cycle production at Robin Hood Street, and by 1895 William had died. However, all had not yet finished with Textiles. A cyclist and motorcyclist by the name of George Hunt, and Charles Campion, got together with a Mill at Milton Works, Milton Street. Here they ran a mill and also had time to develop machinery.
1917. GB 119742A19181017 to do with improvements to stretching and finalising tubular fabrics. Charles William Campion and George Hunt.

1917. A French Patent FR 493166A19190801 improvements to stretching tubular hosiery. Charles William Campion and George Hunt
1918. GB122603A19190130 was similar to the 1917 patent.

1919. Saw another similar patent by the same people, GB142642A19200513 to do with improvements to a calendering mechanism together with GB 159335A19210301.

1922. Another patent with similar improvements was GB203764A19230910.

1924. Was another to do with finishing presses GB230977A1925326 that was also patented in France under FR59423A19250908.

1925. This is the last jointly patented improvement, which will be related to the 1924, but now in Denmark. DE46621919281062.

Some form of hosiery concern, perhaps elastic manufacture, was still in production at Robin Hood Street. Campion's were important in Nottingham not only with improving and building machinery but also providing employment in mills A point previously lost in recent history. During the age of textiles receding in Nottingham, they were still endeavouring to improve production speed, and were easily able to transfer their skills to designing and manufacturing another product, namely the bicycle. This is my 1880's Jones, similar to machines Campion and Newton Wilson produced.

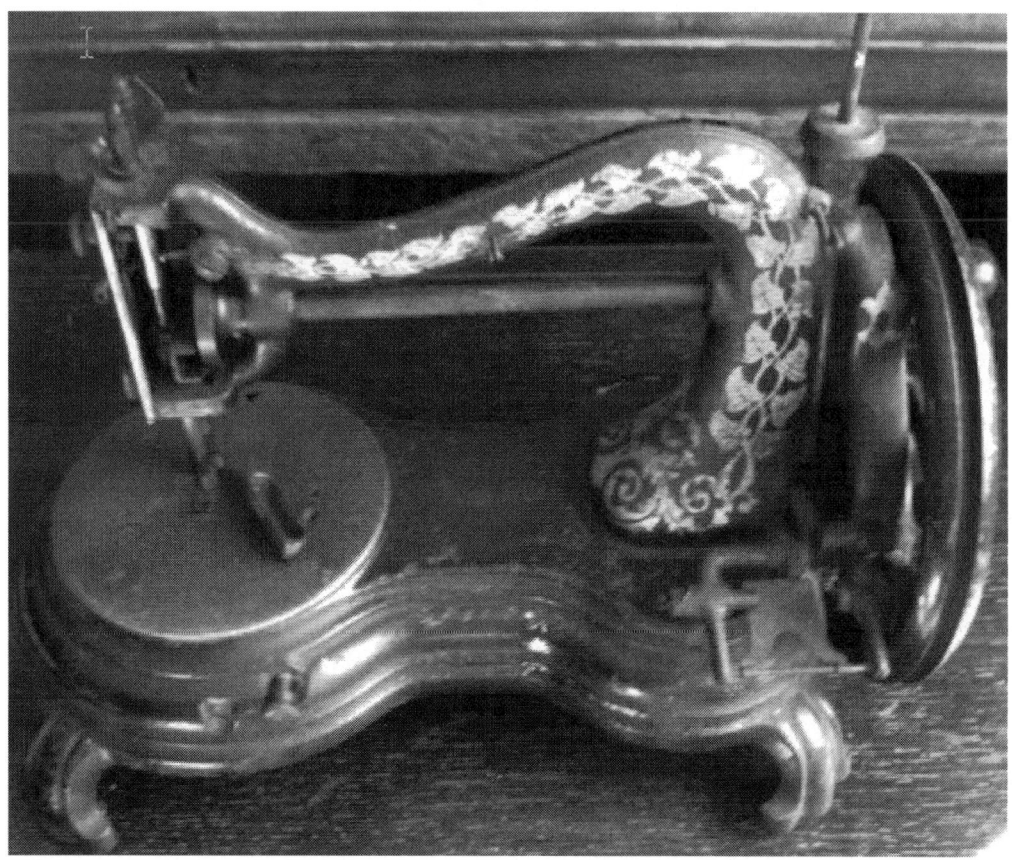

CAMPION FACTORY LOCATIONS

The origins of William Campion arriving in Nottingham, begins with associating himself with Aberdeen St, and Hoyles Factory Woolpack Lane. Here, in a partnership firstly with Mr. Johnson, they established themselves as frame makers and later machine makers. I will discuss other partnerships in associations, but it was at Woolpack lane that the Jenny Lind was patented and textile machinery developed. It cannot be overstressed how important this location was. They were in the heart of the textile trade in Nottingham. They worked here from 1860 to into the 1870`s. The business was sold to Newton Wilson, and later Hind.

This is how this wonderful building, known as Bancroft`s Factory, stands in 2014A great restoration, now divided into flats. This is situated on Liverpool St. To the right is Roden St. Further down Roden St, out of view but added to the end of this building is the Campion section of the factory. The Entrance to Campion`s factory is from Roden St, so the larger building was later divided and kept completely separate.

This is the actual Campion Factory situated at the Junction of Roden St and Liverpool St.

Sadly, not of its former glory.

You can see the importance of the plans lower down.

This is the front. It stands back some few hundred yards.

We have two Plans from the Nottingham Archives, kindly recovered by Brian Binns. These are important for a number of reasons.

The famous Windley's Factory which later became Bancrofts, geographically shows Robin Hood St, Roden Street, and Liverpool Street. All of these Streets appear in paperwork and advertising, giving the impression that there were factories, depots, head offices, all over the place in Nottingham, but as you can see they actually refer to one factory. William Campion did have a couple of cottages at 11 Liverpool Street, but they were used as offices. They actually lived there, as well owning some local pubs!

2 and 4 Carlton Rd, was just around the corner, and was the nearest depot, the next being on Wheeler Gate. Campion's seemed to like the word depot to describe shops.

Advert from 1904. Shops were referred to as depots.

The break down of these plans show individual buildings and what is there within. These are detailed as they were used for insurance purposes dated 1892. It is interesting to see that the factory was built in 1869, and was not divided up till many years later.

From the Windley's Factory, on the East side there is a dotted line dividing the factory to about a third of its total size. This makes it neatly the corner of Roden Street and Liverpool Street. This area was the main Campion Factory for some 40 years.

Look more closely you can see the position of the steam engine and pump room and the chimney. It is clearly marked on these both Hosiery and Cycle Factory. I've included a couple of my own pictures, but what I can't explain or show to you are the vast areas involved, bearing in mind the plans show only one level, where in places there are actually up to four levels. The rest of the factory was converted to flats, and looks a pleasing sight of old verses new in the City.

The different levels of the building are typical mill arrangements of open expanses with wooden floors, supported by cast pillars so typical and wonderful of the period. You can imagine the lay out of the machinery driven by steam from the basement on belts turning flywheels and the clattering of the machinery. Fantastic!

I suspect the cycles and motorcycles were on the ground floor as the period photographs suggest. My father worked at a mill as late as the 1960's, and I can assure you the noise was deafening. People have probably forgot that these ran twenty-four hours a day due to demand and production costs. At night you could see the mills working as they were lit up like Blackpool Tower. Again the noise could be heard from streets away. I remember my father coming home still with cotton wool in his ears after a night shift.

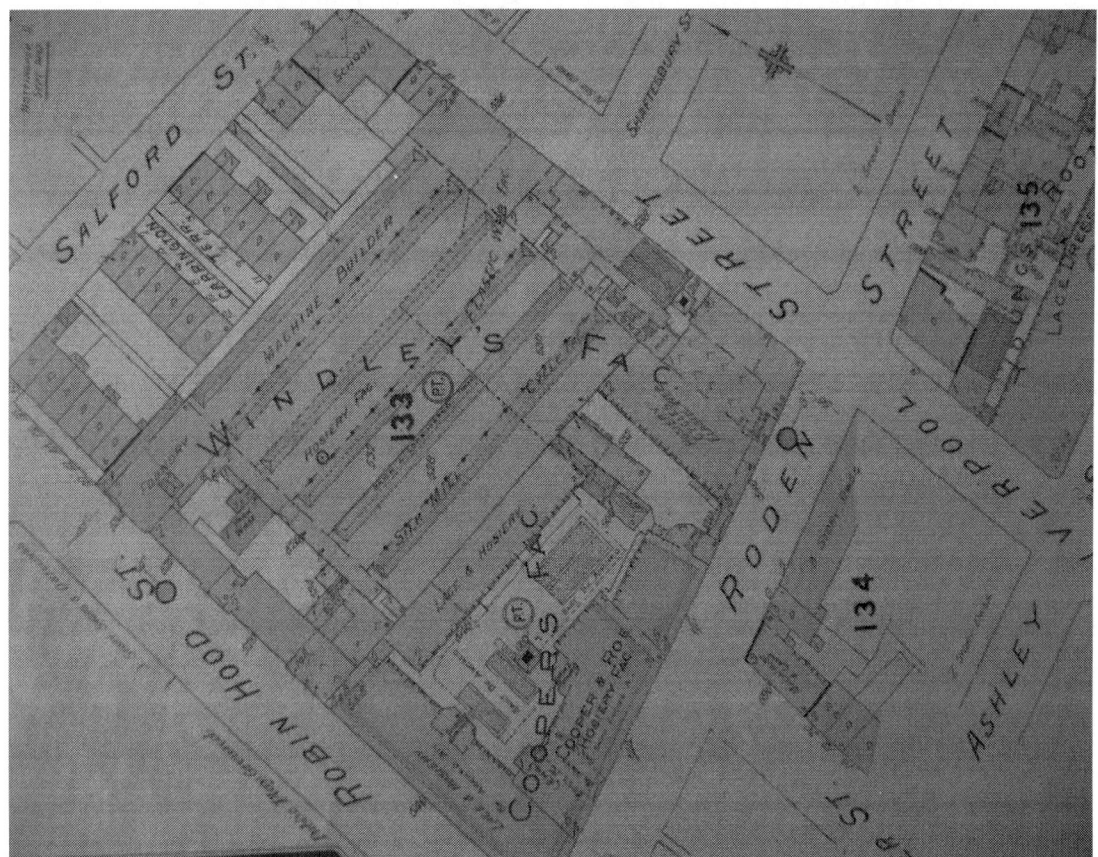

The plan of The Byron Works (named after Lord Byron) situated at the junction of London Rd and the Nottingham Canal, clearly indicates The William Campion Cycle Factory. Thanks to Nottingham Archives for the use of the two plans.

Here, William concentrated purely on the pedal cycles. To date I have found nothing relating to the production of motorcycles other than by a Mr E. Young who became the Bentinck Cycle Co, and was a manager for William regarding puncture repairs and tyre manufacture at this location. He was at London Rd from around 1893, and also sold Campion stock before building his own. For further reading on Mr Young please refer to the Association Chapter.

This plan is dated 1892, and was another grand period building, surrounded by other textile mills, and supporting industry. Now sadly gone. William Campion moved all production from here to expanding Roden St factory in 1895, shortly before he died.

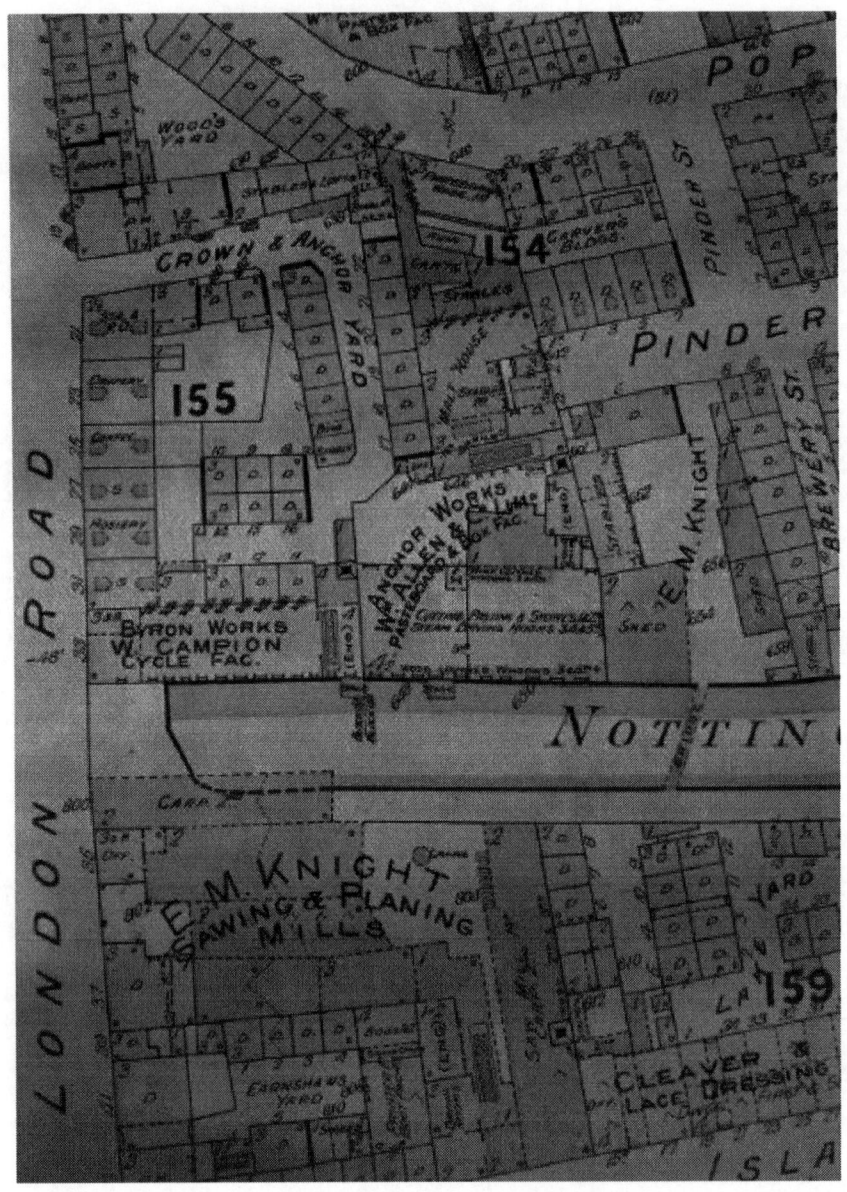

The other interesting fact is that William Campion appears to be edging his bets in producing cycles alongside his textile and hosiery concerns. Could this have incorporated Campion Engineering? This name does crop up, but there are no details as yet. It has still taken another 5 years before the Campion Cycle Company Ltd. was formed in 1897, so during this period what was being engineered? The answer is bicycles. It appears that William referred to the company as the Campion Cycle Co, from around the 1870`s, although it is boasted they had been established since 1855.

At Robin Hood St, they manufactured all forms of bicycles, motorcycles and cars, which they continued through to 1929.

Inside the factory. Present day.

Inside the factory 1919. Thank you to John Beaty for providing this original photo.

Certainly after 1897 things stormed ahead with increased production lead by the new blood of Edwin, and his sons, Charles, Alfred and George Campion, who like their father and his before him, were Engineers. These men were visionaries, taking risks with their own money, coming up with their own ideas, using some others, and making it happen. Above all, they stayed with it.

Campion`s depots included the following 24.

Nottinghamshire.

35 Radford Rd. Between 1892 and 1905.
2-4 Carlton Rd. From 1899.
13 Wheeler Gate.
Leeming Street, Mansfield.
Newark.
Retford.
Sutton in Ashfield.
86 Bridge St, Worksop.
Long Eaton.

Lincolnshire.

Lincoln.
Gainsborough.
Grantham.
Sleaford.

Derbyshire.

Derby.
Station Street, Burton on Trent.
Burlington St, Chesterfield.
Ripley.
Swadlincote.

Edinburgh. From 1899.

London.

Norwich.

70-72 Renshaw Street, Liverpool.

Fargate, Sheffield.

CAMPION BICYCLES

This chapter is a bonus to me, and absolute pleasure to tell you about. Very little if anything is known about Campion Bicycles, other than what is compiled here. I have so many people to thank for background information, history, mechanical detail, and also to the people who allowed me to view the only surviving machines.

William Campion began building the earliest frames and machines himself, possibly with bought in parts. The date when he started is very much up for interpretation. The Nottinghamshire Historical Society state he began in the 1860's. Adverts in the early 1900's suggest he was established from 1855. In Wrights in 1888, we have Edwin Campion and Ernest Hutchinson at 37 Pelham St, listed as bicycle makers. Edwin himself stated that he worked with his father building bicycles. To investigate this further there are a number of other people around at this time to bring the story to life.

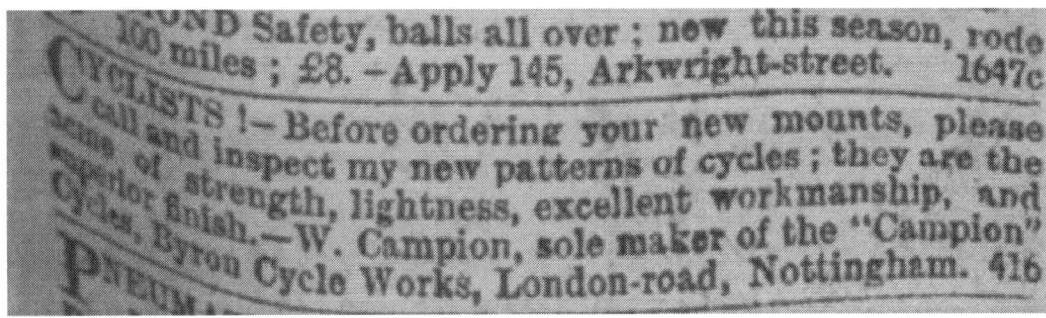

Advert dated 1892. British Newspaper Archives

An advert from 1894 where Mr E.G. Young was acting as manager for Campion at the Byron works shortly to become the Bentinck Motor Co. Please see more on Mr Young in the Association Chapter. Thanks to British Newspaper Archives.

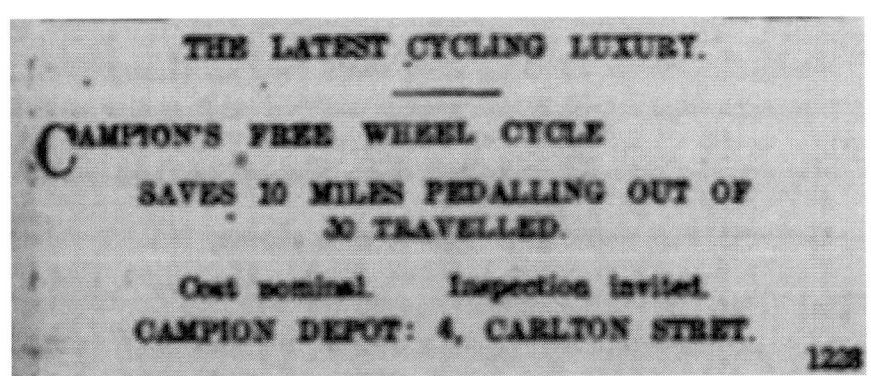

1899 and already advertising.

This must include cycling down hill?

Here we have just one example of advertising the point of being established since 1855. Thanks to the British Newspaper Archives, for the use of the above and this advert.

This advert is from 1899. Note the established since 1855? This date crops up on a number of advertisements into the twenties, questioning bicycle production in its many forms, or was it intended to refer to and include engineering? Note the Finance available, and the other notable statement that the "Machines have not allowed to degenerate from its original standard of excellence." It is worth pointing out the badge. Designed by one of Edwin's sons it was in use from the early 1890`s. The logo Durability, Lightness, speed, and strength, was also used on the motorcycles.
It was only used in a gold transfer form. Two were used on bicycles. On the headstock, and rear mudguard. Whereas only the headstock on motorcycles.

Advert from 1899. Machines were hired. Models included the roadsters, light, safety, and A & B. Thanks to British Newspaper Archives.

Safety, Road Racer, the Quick delivery van. All 1899.

Lets take a look at the earlier years? William Campion and Henry Johnson set up at Hoyles factory in 1859. They had a number of sewing machine patents, but there is no mention of bicycles? The work was concentrating on frames and interlocking sewing machines. Looking into business records we find in 1864, Newton Wilson and Co started manufacturing sewing machines at Hoyles Factory. Newton Wilson, who had factories in London, the Midlands, Manchester and Edinburgh is said to have purchased the Campion Factory, keeping William on to manage it. He more than likely rented it. Here, they made copies of other well-known domestic sewing machines, and exhibited at the Paris Show of 1867. At this show is Michaux Velocipede exhibiting his famous Velocipede. So here we have the possibility that William may have had reason to visit the Paris show with the well-known bicycle maker Thomas Humber, who by now was working as a blacksmith for him. There are no records of Campion exhibiting at Paris.

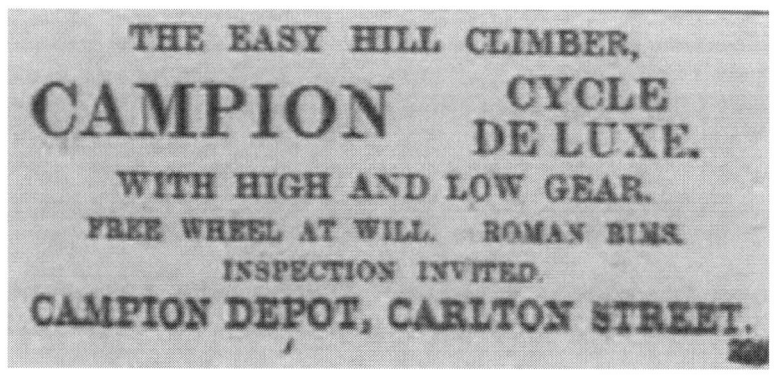

The De Luxe model had a chain guard and mudguards. Livery was chocolate and gold lining. Thanks to BNA.

By 1869, Newton Wilson had established a work force of 500 at London to build Velocipedes. He supplied a Mr Klamroth with such a machine that he rode from London to exhibit at the Edinburgh Show. Was Campion or Humber involved?

Guaranteed for Ever or life was from 1899 as seen and in many other adverts. This one is from the Sheffield depot. Thanks to The British Newspaper Archives.

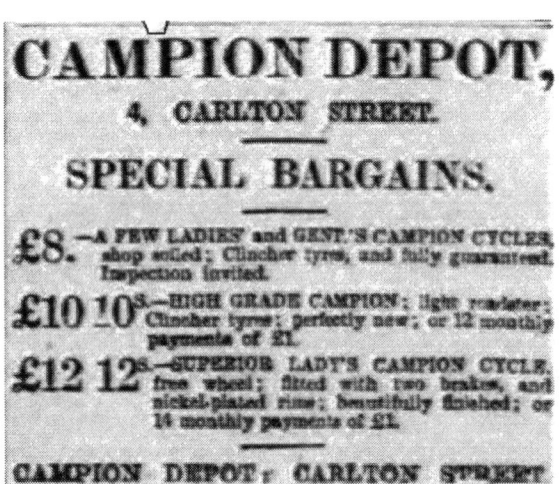

It is well worth mentioning that from 1859 to 1861, James Starley, who needs no introduction, worked for Newton Wilson, repairing sewing machines.

It is well documented that it is Rowley B. Turner who brought back a Velocipede from the same Paris show. Starley copies this with several improvements at Coventry. Coincidence?

He then goes on to make history with his own patents.

Adverts to the left are from 1901 Evening Post With Thanks to the British Newspaper archives.

Discussing the known association of Humber and Campion helps to date their Bicycle production in Nottingham, and throws up some other questions as to their origins? Bear in mind there were only 5 Bicycle manufacturers recorded in Nottingham in the 1880's.

Mr Humber takes credit for a spider bicycle in 1872, but it is clear that later there is a challenge to this with the statement from William Campion that he was responsible for the first spider bicycle in Nottingham? William's son Edwin made this interesting statement. He advertised this every week for a year in 1903. There were no challenges to the accreditation from Mr Humber or a Mr Cooper?

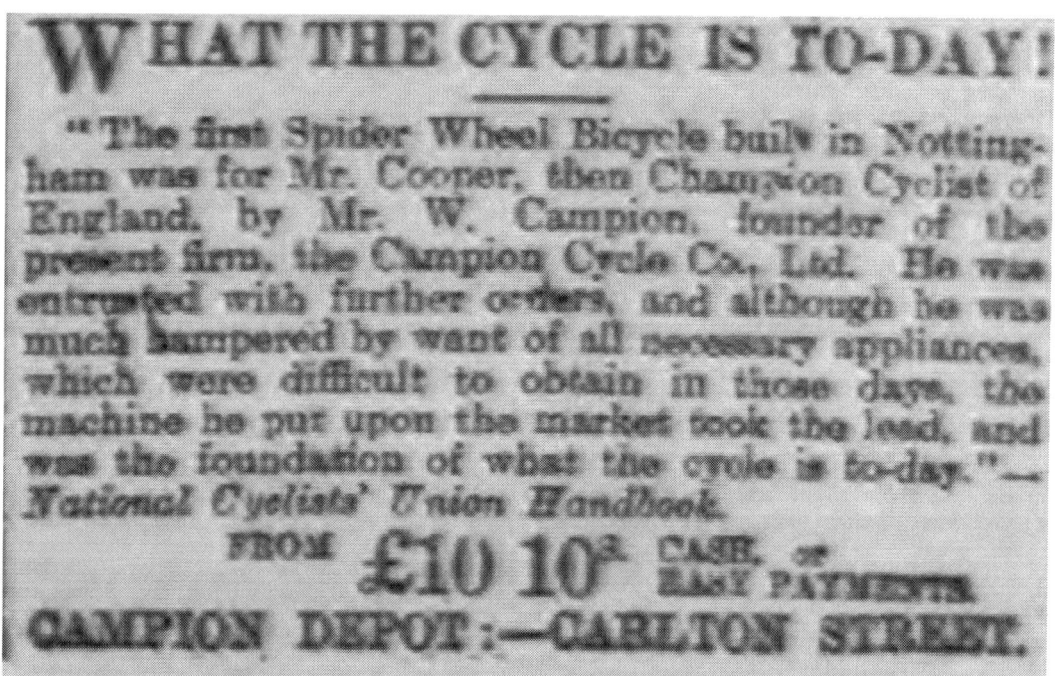

Above is the advert from 1903 that ran every day for a year. There is a lot said in this advert discussed below. Thanks to British Newspaper Archives, and also below.

Advert from 1902. Weights were coming down to under 24lb, and gears were introduced. The free wheel was a Sturmey Archer unit.

The nucleus of bicycle manufacture began in Coventry from about 1869 and spread to other areas there after. As the new fashion developed into a trusty transport for all, William Campion is on the fringes of the initial expanse of the cycle industry. Linked with his associations, he was capable, and prepared to invest. William Campion stated he was responsible for building Nottingham's first Spider Wheel Bicycle. A statement in its self, but he adds that this bicycle was for a Mr F. Cooper, who was a record-breaking cyclist. A boast that Campion stated is covered in the National Cyclists Handbook.

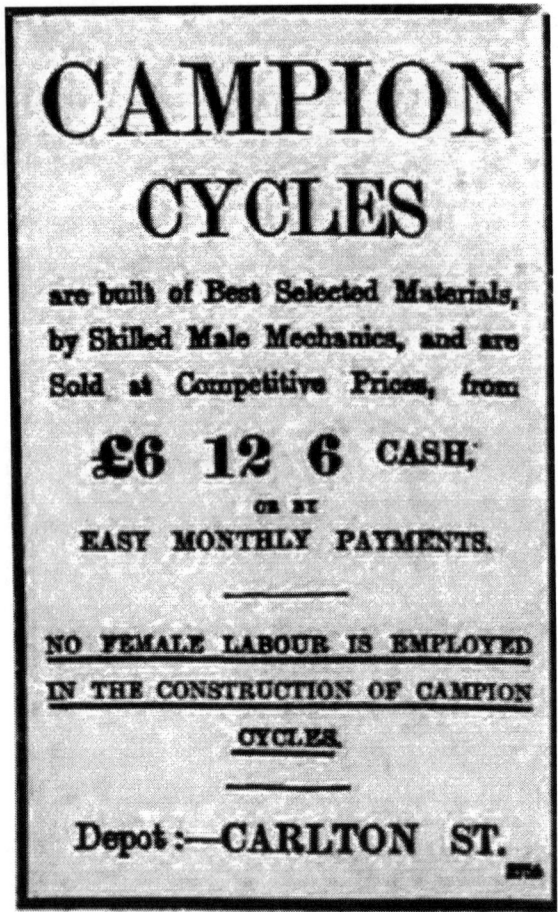

Advert from 1905, which continued for a number of years up to WW1.
The unfair implication of employing women they make clear enough, but it was to change in the factory from 1914.
For very justifiable reasons. Thanks to the British Newspaper Archives.

In 1877, Cooper had joined Marriott and Thomas Humber. By 1885 Cooper and Marriott had left Humber and were retailing cycles made by Rudge, with controversy over the use of the Humber name. One can only assume that if this statement is correct then William could have built the spider before Cooper joined Humber in 1877, whilst Cooper was actively racing. However, Cooper did later set a new record in 1879 for a mile. I do not think that that Mr Humber would have been very pleased for Cooper to be racing a Campion or visa versa. However, if he did build a machine for Cooper, could it have been after Cooper left Humber? This would fit with factory locations, but there is no more information to settle the argument.

The interesting thing is that William Campion is not mentioned in Thomas Humber's own book, but on his daughter's death in 1947, the alliance is discussed. It was stated that William was too busy with sewing machines to make bicycles with Humber. The article also mentions that Thomas copied a French machine making six. Who bought this machine over from Paris we will never know. However there are some choices?

A good period of reference is by machinery patents in 1870 and 1875 at Hoyles. Campion sold the Textile business to Augustine Hine in 1875, so that would be the appropriate time to concentrate on the new bicycle trend. To establish the date as a fact for this is not easy, but you can take into consideration that Spider Wheel Bicycles were around from

1870 until the early 1880's. Another point of interest is that The Robin Hood/Roden Street Factory was not built until 1869, then known as the Windley's Factory and was not occupied by William Campion until after 1873. Here he built textile machinery. Any references of Humber working for Campion 1867/8 at Roden Street are therefore not possible?

It is clear that William Campion was unlikely to have been established in 1855 with building bicycles, despite their claims. However, he was established from that time in designing and building textile machines. William sold most of his textile machinery in auction from the Windley's site in 1878, but kept the building. What did he do with it? He stated he was retiring from the textile business? Bicycles went into production as a small concern around 1878. He could have built tricycles and quads during an earlier period but I can find nothing as yet to substantiate this. I have found evidence to suggest that bicycles were built in the mid 1880's and onwards, in conjunction with his son Edwin, and Ernest Frederick Hutchinson. They were using 37 Pelham Street as an outlet that continued up to 1930. Mr Hutchinson was to become a partner in 1897 of The Campion Cycle Company Ltd. Interestingly he inherited into the textile business through his father who owned the fine mill on Russell Street. Ring any bells? Raleigh in its earlier days rented a part of this building as a part of its early expansion.

At the Robin Hood Street factory a modest cycle production was there before 1880. At their height production rose to 400 bicycles a week, and were exported all over the world. The manager was Edwin. Also involved were his sons George, Charles and Alfred. Bicycles were built, that evolved into forecars, motorcycles and light cars. This alliance of textiles and machinery, continued into the mid 1920's.

The textile trade was a very important mainstay of the company. I have only found outside investment in 1897 and 1922. Unlike other similar companies, Campion stuck together as a family and as a business, trading as simply Campion, and Campion Cycles. Edwin formed the Campion Cycle Company Ltd in 1897 after William's death, which remained an established name in Nottingham right up to 1930.

Not only traditional styled bicycles were built, but competition machines including racers and tricycles. Tricycles were established earlier in a trade format, in that they were built with two wheels at the front to enable carrying goods. Called fast vans, they were adapted with an engine. See further details in Chapter relating to cars and motorcycles. De Dion were established in 1895 with a sturdy single cylinder mounted at the rear driving two wheels, that were copied by various companies. The Campion engine was possibly like this. The front therefore had two wheels. This initially was marketed for factory use, almost the first mobile fork lift! Its uses were varied before carrying people. Humber, Raleigh and Campion also built them and they became a regular sight on a Sunday, heading for Trent Bridge, and lovers walk? If you could not to own one, you could rent a machine from Jardines. Recognise the name? He had everything from bicycles to a steam bus for rent.

The Quick delivery van was widely used by various tradesmen, and was to become the fast van when an engine was added. BNA.

An original picture of 1899, donated by Mr Beaty showing a Campion Van at work. The rider is holding to a handle bar fitted to the van. This is pivoted on the centre of the axle, and was mounted on springs. I have not come across the term "Van" used in this context before? Did they invent it? It did continue to identify light goods vehicles.

Competition was an important part of advertising and development. Campion sponsored racing with local clubs. The Campion Challenge Shield was a regular event with the Castle Club, of which Alfred Campion, did rather well in local racing and formed a friendship with a Mr Young, competing on Tandems. See further details in Associations. Also a competitive rider was Charles Campion, son of Edwin who was formerly of Nottingham High School.

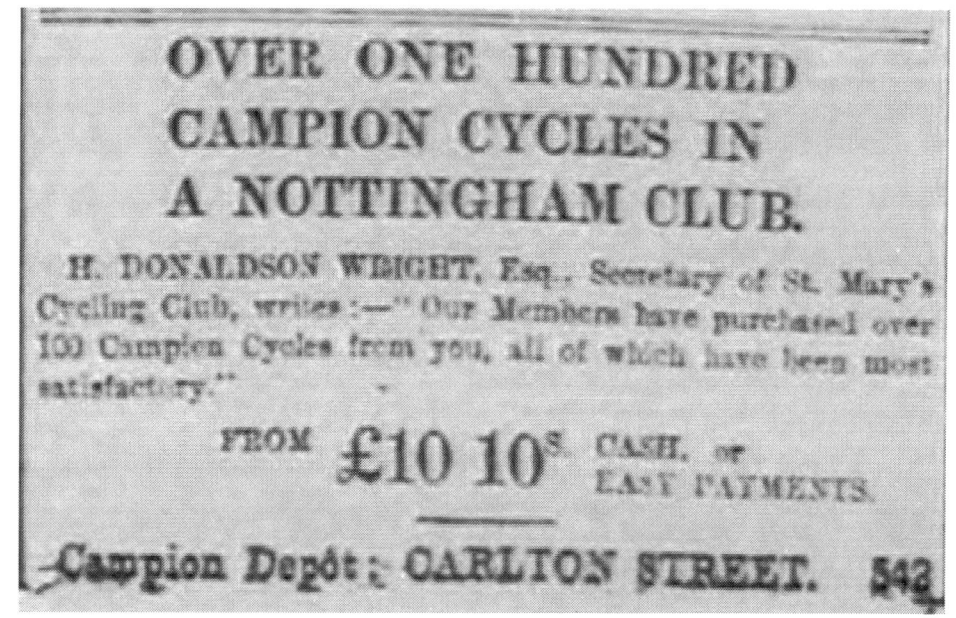

A 1903 Advert showing the popularity of cycle clubs. The Nottingham Cycle Club, The Mechanics, and the Castles Clubs to name a few. BNA.

One of the most interesting racing machines were the Tandems. Campion built these in racing trim or touring trim.

A Campion tandem. This is dated around 1900. Thank you to the Nottingham Historical Film Unit and Picture the Past Organisation for this only example.

Even during production, 1905 Campion could still make a special, built to order machine. Possibly with racing in mind?

A great Sturmey-Archer Advert for the three-speed gear. Some other Nottingham makes, Triumph, Robin Hood, are there and also Mead, who features in The Curry's take over. Interestingly there is no mention of Curry? Thanks to the BNA.

Campion did not build their own-geared hubs, but used mainly SA, with whom they had a long relationship continuing with motorcycle production. The motorcycles fitted with none geared hubs, were all made in house, along with frames, tanks, etc.

There were around 25 models by 1911. Here are but a few of racing machines that naturally came in all sizes for ladies or gents, and children. Interestingly, prices have halved in ten years. Thanks to the BNA.
It is very difficult to name and describe models, but we are fortunate to have a few original machines photographed. I have also included a very rare catalogue. Great thanks go to the Veteran Cycle Club for their help.
See below.

These following pages are from the 1913 Wheeler Gate Campion Catalogue.
Frames were designed to carry persons no heavier than 16 stone. That's me out of it then?
Below and for the next few pages I have taken extracts to show the various designs.
This is only a small amount of information, preserved and available to us, by the Vintage Cycle Club. My thanks to them for their help, advice, and the work they put in to saving and protecting original documents and machinery for us to enjoy.

Campion Cycles

BALL BEARINGS.—These are, to all intents and purposes, absolutely dust-proof; hubs, cups, cones, and balls are made of the finest steel procurable, and are such as will sustain that splendid reputation which the CAMPION Cycles have obtained for their easy-running and lasting qualities. The bearings are made by automatic machinery, and their accuracy is guaranteed. We fit to order the Sturmey-Archer Tri-Coaster Hub at a charge of £1 7 6; also the celebrated Eadie Coaster Hub, the B.S.A., or Sturmey-Archer Three-Speed Gear. These specialities are well known, and guaranteed by the makers.

Campion Cycles

HANDLE BARS.—We fit the following Handle Bars to our Machines: No. 1, North Road, 2½ in. drop, 18 in. wide; No. 2, Racing, 4 in. drop, 15 in. wide; No. 3, Flat, 16 in. wide; No. 5, Upturned, 16 in. wide; and each one may be fitted instead of the one shown in the illustration of machine. Our customers, in order to obtain suitable Handle Bars, should give the number of Handle Bar required.

TOOL BAGS.—All CAMPION Cycles are sent from works fitted complete, including tool bag, two spanners to fit all nuts, and an oil can. The SPECIAL CAMPIONS are fitted with a tool bag as illustrated, containing a full complement of tools. Attached to the outside is a card case for name and address, which will be found useful when travelling by rail.

Campion Cycles

BRAKES.—We have always regarded the brake as a most important adjunct of a cycle, and great care has been taken to design a brake which can be relied upon.

The Roller-lever brake is very efficient, and all the parts being exposed, is easy for adjustment. The concealed roller brakes are actuated by a lever which passes through the handle bar, giving a smart, neat appearance to the machine. The weight has been reduced to a minimum.

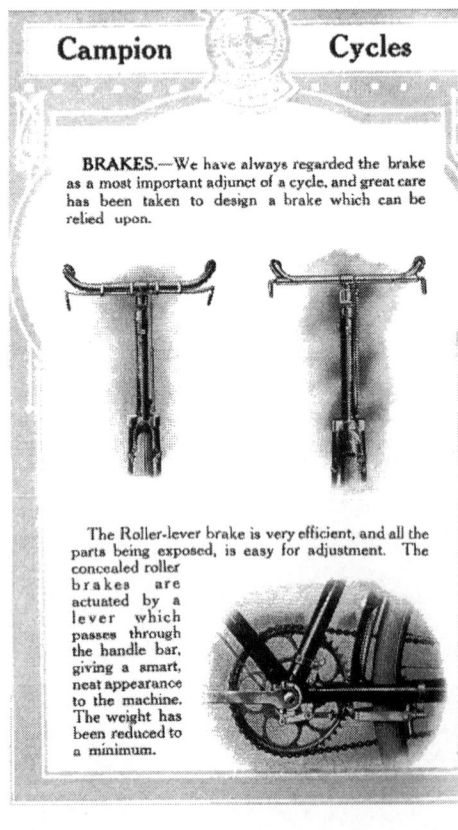

Campion Cycles

TYRES.—To meet the requirements of our customers, we are prepared to fit any standard tyre ordered. From experience we recommend Dunlop Tyres, and, unless otherwise ordered, we fit them to nearly all our models. We can supply Dunlop Tyres with a beaded or wired edge as desired. Dunlop quality is so well known, and their guarantee so liberally interpreted, that it is unnecessary to enlarge upon their merits.

STEERING LOCK.—Near the head is illustrated our new Steering Lock, which is a steel band round the fork stem, actuated by a large milled nut. It cannot be lost, and is effective without being a positive lock.

GEAR CASE.—This is an excellent gear case, giving perfect chain protection, which is oil-retaining for the lubrication of the chain, and celebrated as the Campion oil-bath gear case.

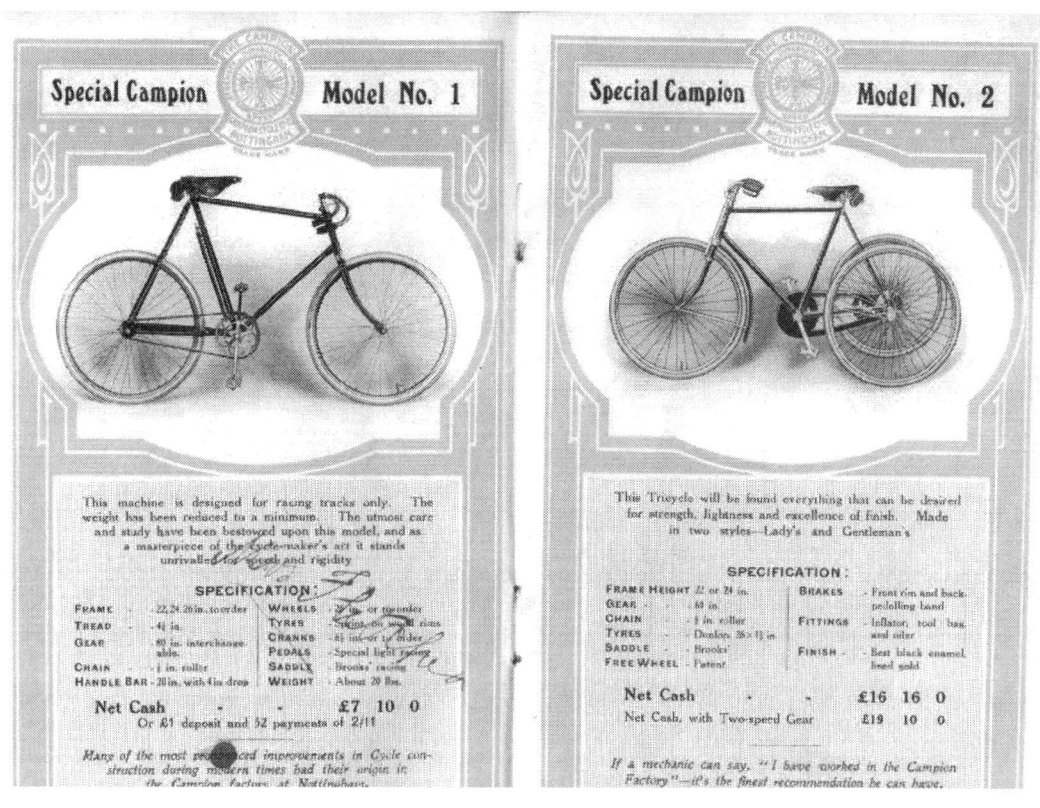

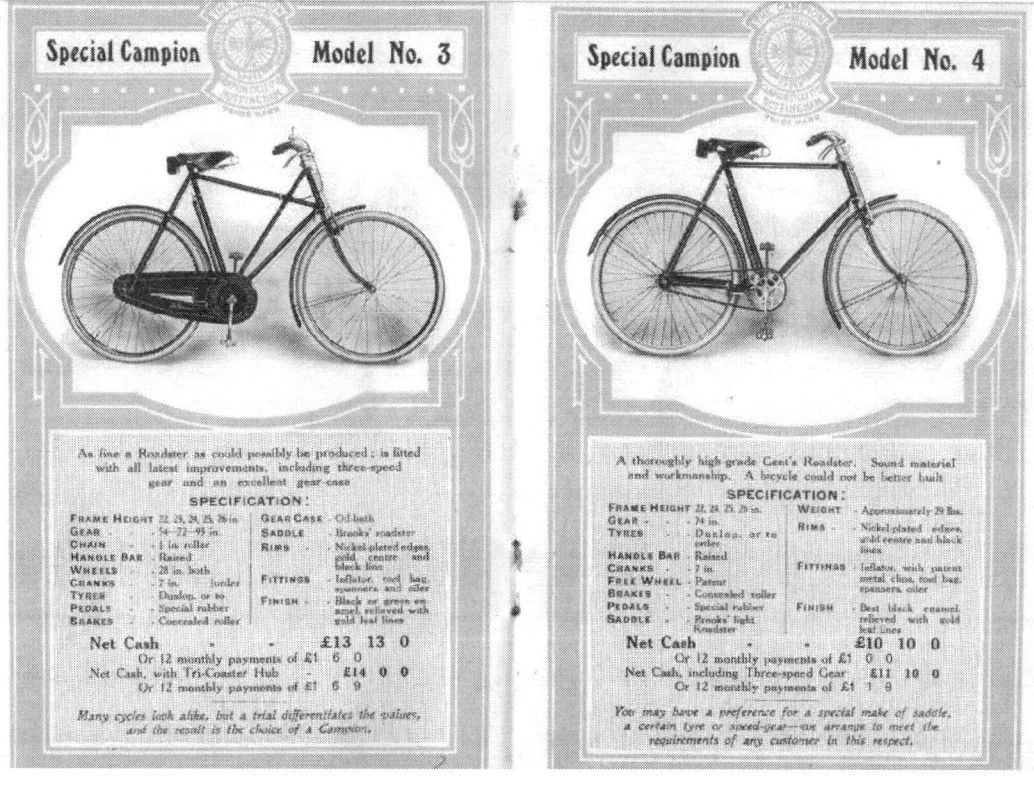

28

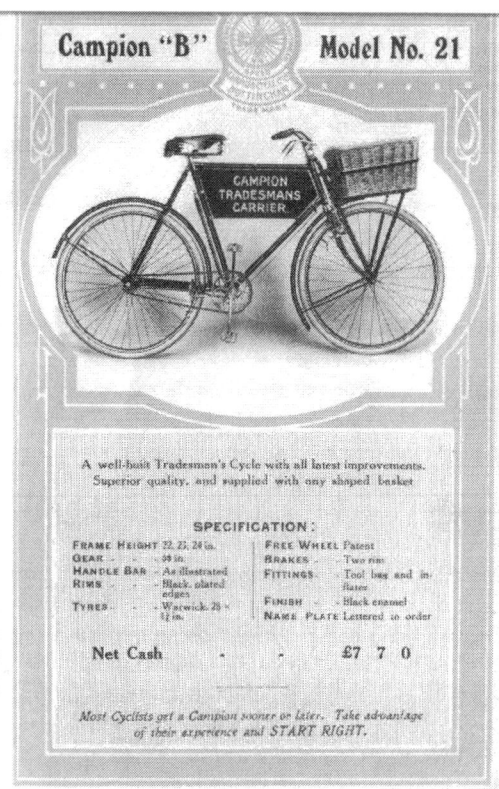

The photograph overleaf is again from the collection of the VCC. This is from a diary of photographs taken around 1900 by the Nottingham Cycle Club on their adventures, and a sample of documents stored there.

I am very honoured to include here the wonderful and rare bicycles belonging to Mr Caldwell, and Mr Jackson.

To those of you who are very knowledgeable of bicycles I hope you will appreciate the engineering of these rare machines. I hope everyone else enjoys them and can see their quality described in 1900 at the Nottingham Cycle Show as "maintaining their reputation for finish and general excellence."

Above is a 1920`s machine. Metal rims. Note the Campion Transfer on rear Mudguard, period carrier, and provision for lighting. The seat was fitted from 1899 for a number of years and can be misleading on the date of the machine.

Below is a view of the forks and brakes, typical of the period. Nice chromed bottom yoke. Stirrup brake. You can still see the hand coach lines in green. Adjustable chain.

The rear brake is a rod arrangement and nicely pivoted through the frame to give more support and strength.

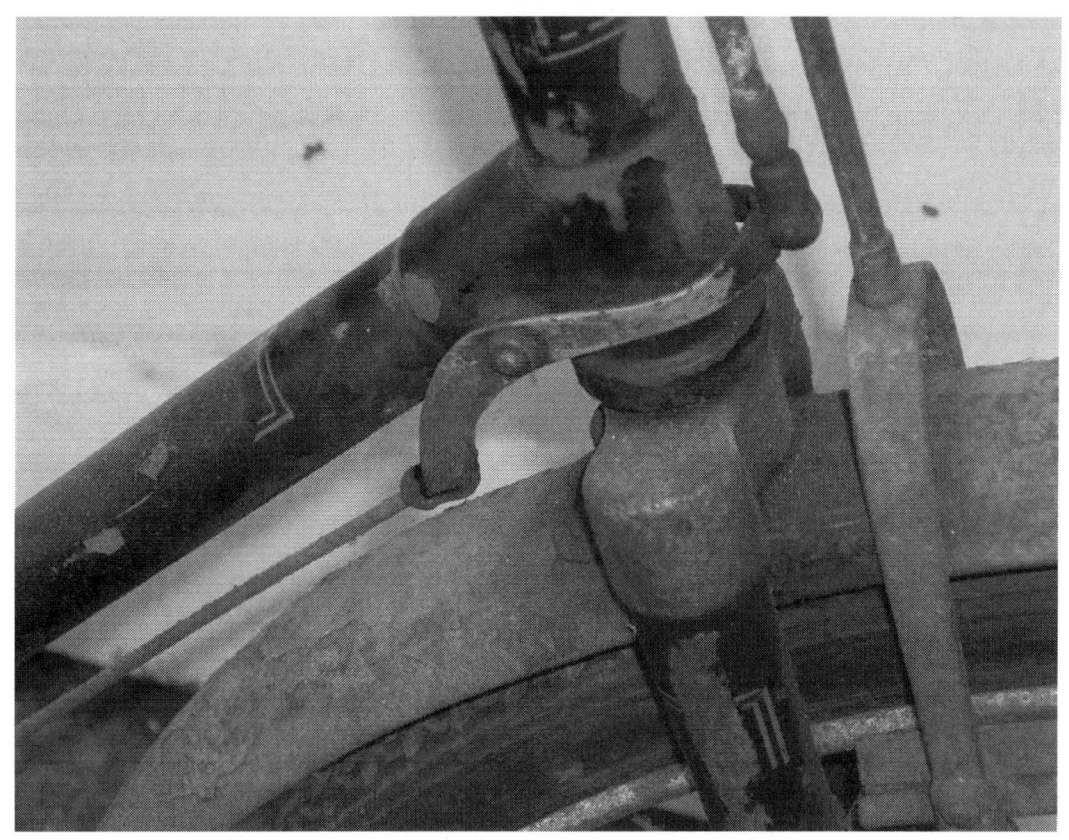

Above is an original gents Campion racer or tourer model 1. Date possibly 1895. Note the transfer on rear mudguard. All machines have these. Adjustable chain. Wooden rims and clincher tyres. Still usable today and with a great front brake.

If I say so myself, great pictures of this machine showing the diamond frame, Sturmey-Archer two speed hub, and leather tool bag, complete with original spanners.

Below are some shots of a Campion Special number 3. The leather tool carrier on the saddle still has the Campion emblems there on. Note the levers integral with the bars, and a thumb gearshift. This is dated 1912 and is a one-owner machine.

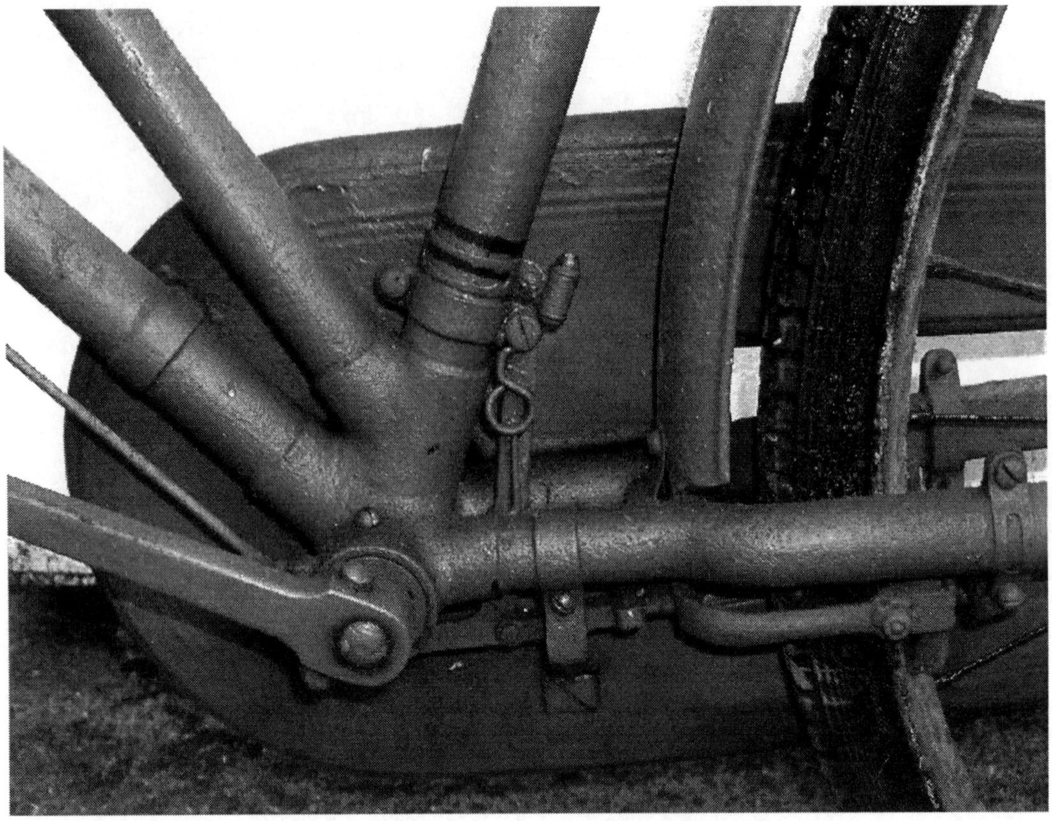

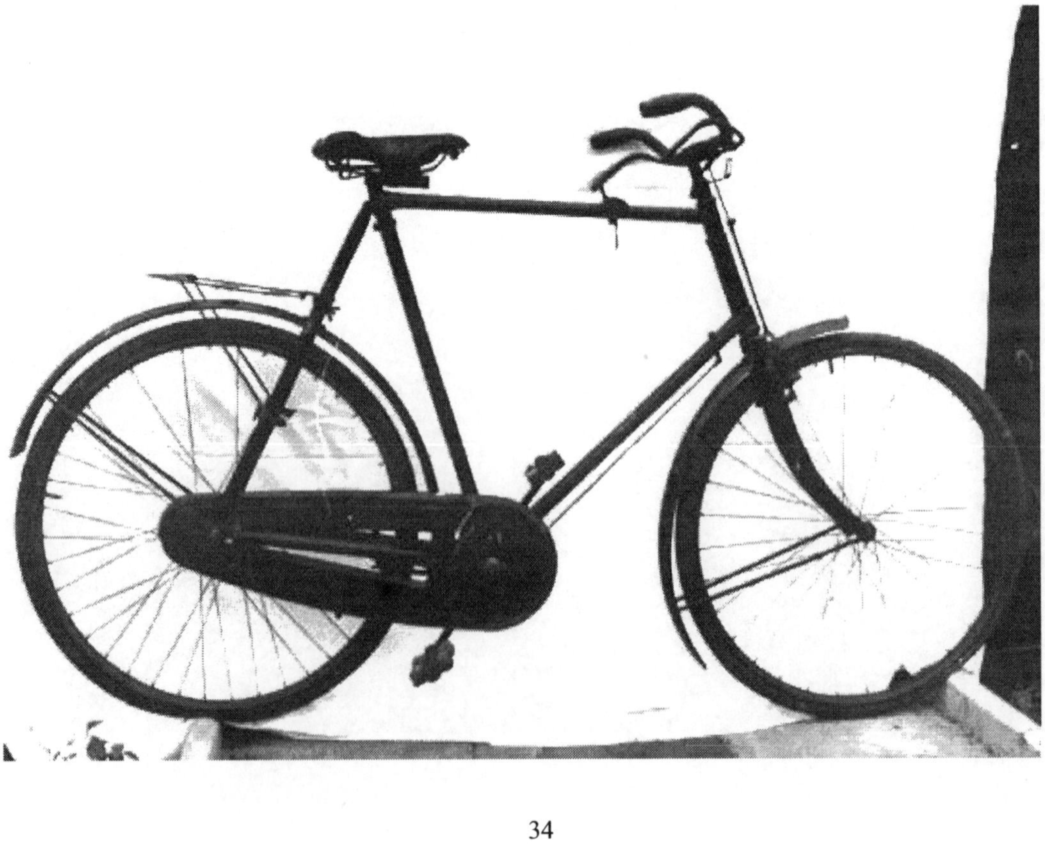

A Tourer from the 1920's belonging to Mr Jackson. Full mudguards and chain case, steel rims, and split pedals, SA three speed. Good view of the bolt up crank and rear brake linkage.

Wonderful Ladies step through dated about 1920. Below the bolt up crank.

View of double pressing rear frame and adjustable chain, and free wheel hub.

View of pressed double fork blades. A copy of Humber's? Or is this dating it before their patent? We will never know, but a great example of frame building.

Before finishing off this chapter I should mention that Campion produced these machines till 1928. Numerous new parts were built up to sell during the Curry's (ltd) 1927 takeover, lasting until 1930, but still being seen in 1933.

George Campion in 1929, immediately set up building his own cycles, called G.F. Campion Cycles.

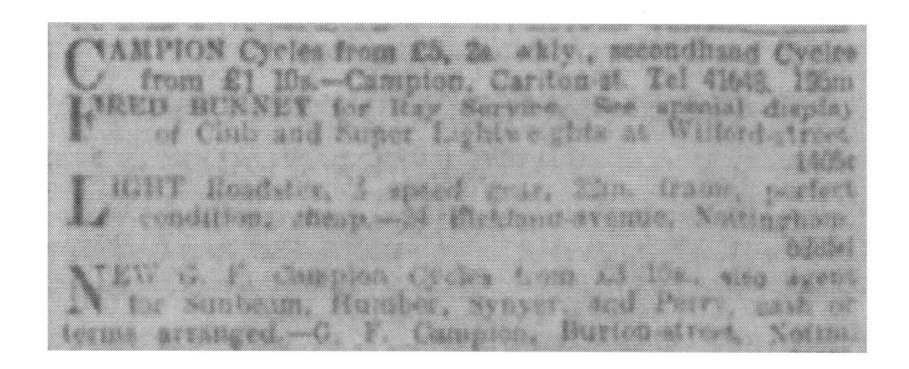

This 1929 advert shows Curry's advertising Campion machines, and Georges Campion's new business. At the same time, George's father Edwin, had set up on Station Street with second hand Campion motorcycles, and also as a BSA agent. Thanks to the BNA for this.

I have included a number of shows attended by William Campion and then as The Campion Cycle Company.

1893 Nottingham Exhibition. W. Campion and J.H. Ford.
A Bicycle named the Strathmore for the Scottish market at the Dundee Show.
1898 Stanley Show. 21 Bicycles were displayed including 3 tandems.
1899 Stanley Show. All 25 Bicycles exhibited were sold, with reference to Tandems.
1900 Nottingham Cycle Show. Displayed bicycles with back pedalling brakes.
1901 Nottingham Cycle Show.
1902 Nottingham Show.
1902 Stanley Show.

CAMPION MOTORCYCLES

This has taken quite a while to compile and attain accuracy. Using the few catalogues available, lists from the Red Book, details of models (kindly provided from Beaulieu) and from countless adverts collated from 1900 through to 1929. I have included show appearances as there are many show reports which describe in detail, changes from year to year. The list of shows included, are at the end of the chapter.

The earliest factory photo of 1904. Thanks to the Nottingham Historical Film Unit and Picture the Past for the use of this. Note the forecar/sidecar at rear, and own engine right.

It is suggested that Campion fitted Fafner Engines in the early years but I have not found an example. It is clear that the first true motorcycle consisted of an engine under slung on little more than a standard bicycle frame, the first being their own engine in 1899. This was also used in the forecar, and later superseded by a Minerva in 1902. This rapidly progressed with larger bought in engines. Everything else was built in house. The following is a break down of the innovation and progression of the motorcycles up to 1928. I have complied a detailed year-by-year reference list at the end of the Chapter, which refers to engines, years and models. There are overlaps with the Car and Sidecar Chapters.

Campion's first appearance of significance at a trade show was the 1911 Leicester Show. Displayed was a well-presented Peugeot engined 2-speed Roc geared machine, primarily intended for sidecar work. Also here was H. Curry presenting the J.A.P engine machine

in a diamond frame together with Campion. This was never seen again?
In 1912, again at Leicester Campion displayed the J.A.P 4hp and Peugeot 3 ½ hp engine machines with Roc 2 speed gears. Also here was the Villiers 2 stroke engine with free engine hub. Introduced for the first time is the Campion TT model. This model with a J.A.P 4hp engine had a free engine hub.

Above and below we have an early Precision model belonging to Joe Rush

A good view of the Precision Engine and the quadrant gear change lever leading to a Jardine 2-speed gearbox. The silencer remained the same other than changing to the other side for the pipe, until production ceased. The flat footplates were typical of those fitted to Campion machines until 1913/14 when the aluminium sledge style, were fitted to all models except the TT which had pegs like most modern machines.

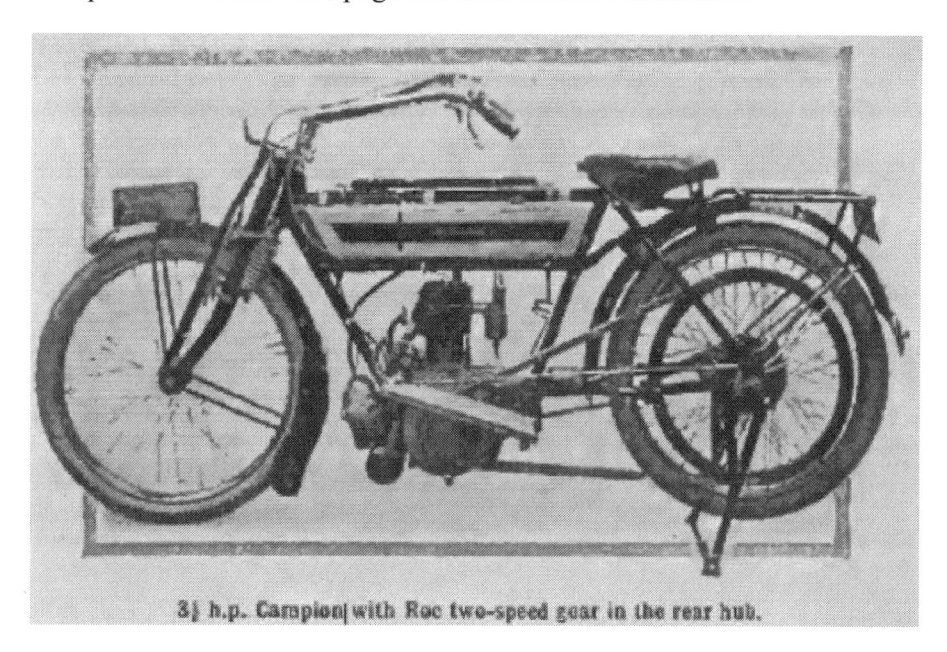

3½ h.p. Campion with Roc two-speed gear in the rear hub.

Thanks to TCM Publication for the use of these.

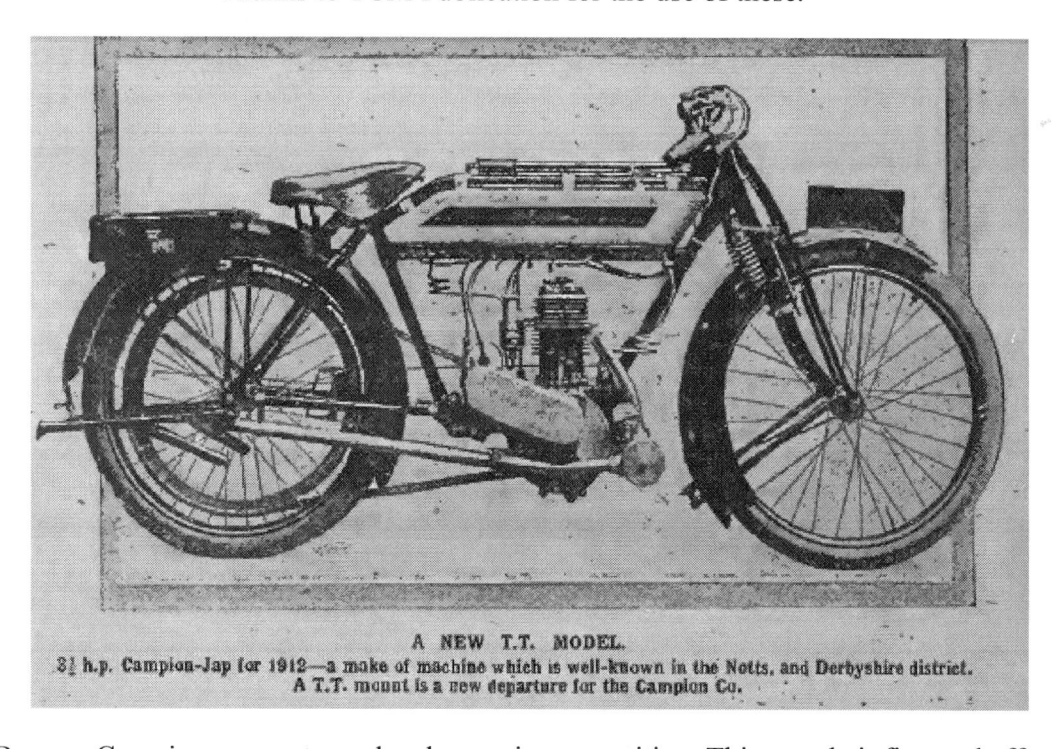

A NEW T.T. MODEL.
3½ h.p. Campion-Jap for 1912—a make of machine which is well-known in the Notts. and Derbyshire district. A T.T. mount is a new departure for the Campion Co.

By now Campion was a strong local name in competition. This was their first real effort

41

of a competition production machine. The frame is of lighter tubing, and the wheelbase slightly shorter. The exhaust was replaced with a straight through system. Mr E. Briggs rode this model with the drop bars, to many successes, even against geared models.

Great pictures of a well-known machine, which has been ridden to many events.

This was Phillip Jackson's excellent 1912 4hp J.A.P machine, with a pedal start that finished this year. You can easily see the gear change going straight to the rear 2-speed hub. The livery was typical of the period and discontinued from late 1914. Earlier colour schemes included aluminium as well as black with gold lining which continued to well after the war.

The Motor Cycle Gear for 1914 The Famous

STURMEY-ARCHER

3-Speed & Free Engine Gear

will be fitted by the following firms as a **standard specification** of their 1914 motor cycles—	will be fitted by the following firms to their 1914 models, **to order**—
TRIUMPH	RUDGE-WHITWORTH
HUMBER	PREMIER
BRADBURY	SINGER
ROVER	ALLDAYS & ONIONS
ARIEL	HAZLEWOOD
SWIFT	BROWN
EXCELSIOR	O.K.
CALCOTT	RAGLAN
CAMPION	IXION
HOBART BIRD	IMPERIAL
SUN	VELOCE
JAMES	WULFRUNA
L.M.C.	QUADRANT
A.J.S.	MOTO-REVE
IVY-PRECISION	
ROYAL RUBY	
VICTORIA	

New booklet post free—
STURMEY-ARCHER GEARS, LTD., NOTTINGHAM.
OLYMPIA, STAND 159 (Gallery).

Campion used SA as well as Jardine gearboxes, Fitted throughout the range. Thanks to TCM publications

1913 was an important year for Campion in that it was their effort to launch nationally at Olympia, stand 20. Displayed were a variety of machines the larger demonstrating the strength of the sidecar and quality finish. They were already making a name for themselves in competition, which was mentioned.

The first model being a J.A.P 5hp V-Twin 76 x 85mm engine, B & B Carburettor with the Jardine 3-speed gearbox. Chain drive with kick-start. The machine was pale grey with green lining. The sidecar matched with green leather upholstery and a watertight cover. The chassis of the sidecar being very strong with the rear C springs being enclosed within the body. There is room for a luggage carrier on the rear.

The second model was a J.A.P 8hp V-Twin 85 x 85mm engine, B & B Carburettor, with 3-speed Jardine gearbox. Chain drive. Kick-start.

The Third model was an 8hp V-Twin Precision engine with three speed Jardine gearbox and chain driven through out. The Gearbox is the new countershaft, its gears easily selected with use of a quadrant on the tank. On top of the gearbox is a large oiler. Attached to the machine is a sidecar described as "Exceedingly graceful" in its appearance. It was painted in a French Grey with matching coach lines, fitted with a carrier for luggage.

A show machine in French Grey matching lining and lots of plating, typical of show machines. TCM.

Lastly was a Green- Precision (water-cooled) 3 ½ hp 85 x 88mm, Jardine 2-speed gearbox, chain driven, with a neat water tank fitted to the top tube to allow for evaporation. The display was described as "a striking one".

1914 was the introduction of Jardines all new 4-speed countershaft gearbox with kick-start. It went straight into Mr George Hunts Competition machine that won many awards, thereby suitably testing the gearbox. Most recorded references to Campion for the war period state they were inactive, however it is surprising what they did get up to, as well as aircraft parts.

This was George Hunts machine. Note the cast Footplates now fitted. Thanks to TCM Publications.

The 8 h.p. Campion, fitted with Jardine four-speed gear, on which our tests were made.

Still another Gold Medal for the CAMPION.

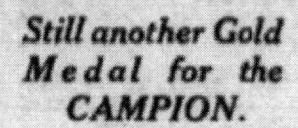

In the A.C.U. 6 days trial, motor cycle and side-car class, which concluded last Saturday, the highest award GOLD MEDAL was won by the all-conquering

CAMPION

However much more you may pay, (and you can pay considerably more) you cannot get a more reliable motor-cycle than the CAMPION.

Call at one of our depots, and arrange a trial run

Pelham St., Carlton St., and Wheeler Gate, Nottingham

---

man with clean hands

When you see a motor-cycle spinning along a country road, you think "Fine fun, but too complicated a business for me."

In course of time you get a motor-cycle catalogue, which you find brimful of details about carburetters, magnetos, clutches, and plugs

and you throw it down like the small boy does his Greek grammar, and go on with the dear old push bike

Now the motor-cycle is not at all the terrible thing you think it is. In fact you would be just as happy and confident as the hundreds of other men you see riding.

The best thing you can do is to call at a Campion Depot and have a chat with one of the assistants, and if you like, arrange a trial run. A little practical demonstration will soon show you that there is nothing to be afraid of after all, and you'll come away laughing at your former lack of confidence.

CAMPION
the reliable

FOR THE NOVICE
(as well as the expert rider)

The best motor-cycle is the Campion

Because the whole of its mechanism can be understood in an hour, and it is so easy to control

Call at one of our depots and arrange a trial run— it commits you to nothing

CAMPION
the reliable
Pelham St., Carlton St. and Wheeler Gate

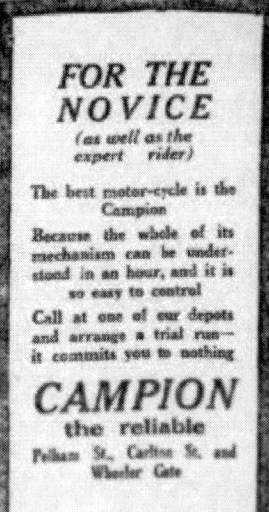

The CAMPION is the motor-cycle for those glorious non-stop runs

A local man writes: "I have done more than 3,500 miles on my CAMPION and have not once been held up on the road for any mechanical trouble whatever."

And you could do it too

It is so comfortable

Built very low, with easy saddle and rubber-covered footboards.

No work, no fatigue, no dismounting to adjust this or that. You just sit still and "let her go".

CAMPION
motor-cycle
the luxury of a luxurious age

Nottingham depots—Carlton St. and Wheeler Gate

Adverts from the period that cover all aspects of a great machine. Including Reliability, Comfort, Success in Competition, and importantly, easy to maintain?

Thanks to The British Newspaper Archives for their use.

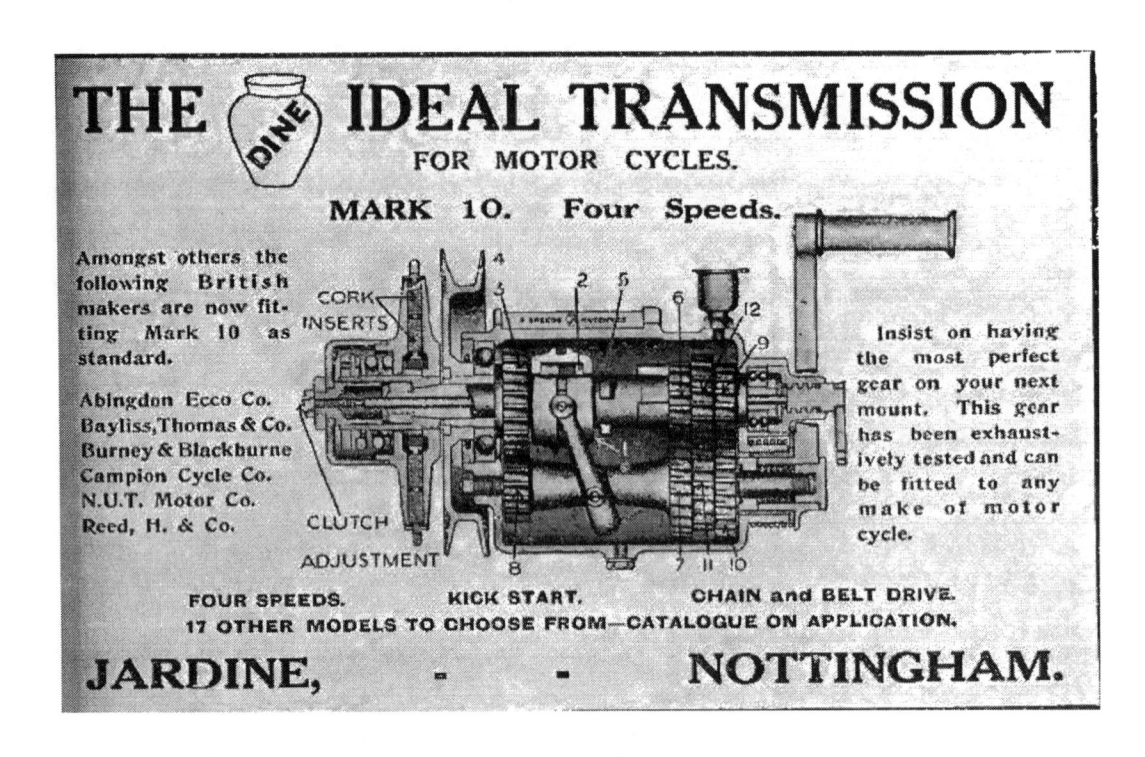

Chain options were always available but you could also choose an engine to suit.

This is Len Kelly's early J.A.P 8hp machine with Sturmey-Archer 3-speed gearbox undergoing a great restoration in Australia.

1916 brought two heavyweights to the public, both 8hp and 4-speed in Khaki Livery, along with two stroke singles. Stronger frames were fitted to the sidecars with four-point fixing.

The two-stroke Campion which is fitted with a two-speed gear and chain-cum-belt drive. As will be gathered from this illustration alternative tank finishes are offered by the makers.

A high-powered sidecar mount—the new 8 h.p. twin-cylinder Campion—which has all chain drive and a Jardine four-speed gear. All chains have cases, but when photographed the latter were removed.

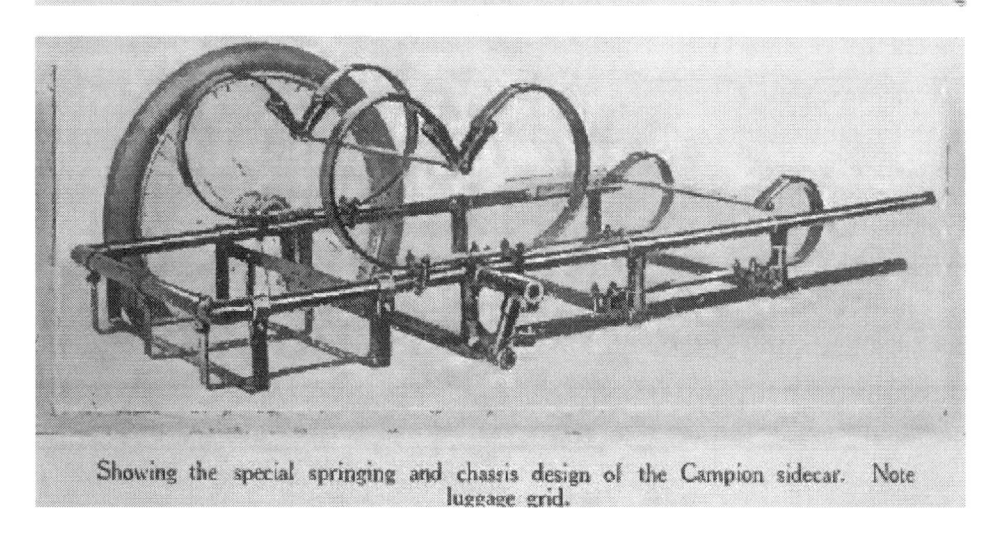

Showing the special springing and chassis design of the Campion sidecar. Note luggage grid.

The four-stroke Campion lightweight. The engine is a 2¼ h.p. J.A.P., and a two-speed countershaft gear in conjunction with chain-cum-belt drive is adopted

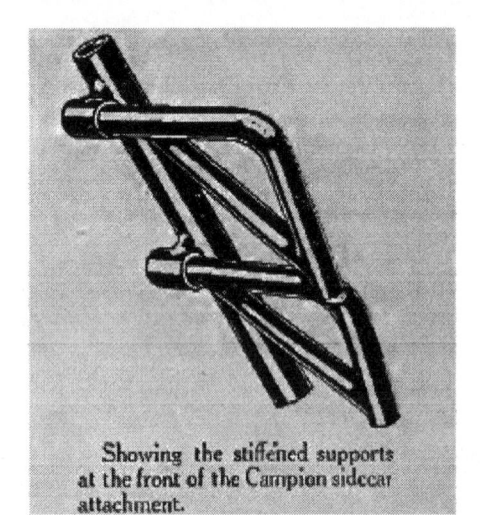

Showing the stiffened supports at the front of the Campion sidecar attachment.

The improvements to fixing the sidecar to the motorcycle were substantial, and no doubt learned from lessons in competition. Thanks to TCM Publications.

Campion claimed the rear end was removed by undoing only three wing nuts. This gave access to the rear wheel. The toolboxes, as well as a clasp and buckle, had magnets at either end of the top cover to keep the ends closed.

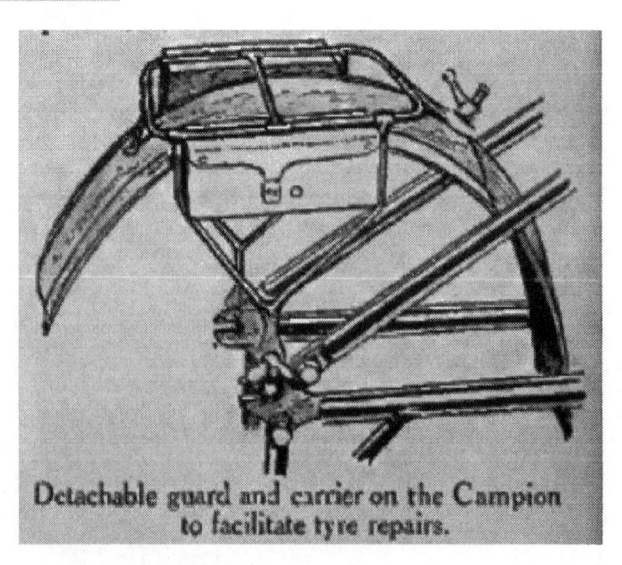

Detachable guard and carrier on the Campion to facilitate tyre repairs.

This year on the rear of the sidecar an unusual 7 ¼ inch internal expanding Ferodo lined brake is offered, whilst retaining the front rim brake. This is foot operated by a toggle lever movement. The all chain drive was fully enclosed in a aluminium case.
There were the all-new Druids fitted, incorporating additional springs fitted above the fork crown. The carburettor fitted was the pilot jet B & B, where as the two stroke used an Amac.

There was also a foot change offered for the Jardine gearbox, and an Albion 2-speed gearbox for the lightweights. The oil tank had an Enots clear feed fitted.

A valuable point for the comfort of the rider was made about the angled cast foot plates that offered toe and heal support because of the raised front.

A high-powered machine—the 8 h.p. twin-cylinder Campion—which, with its Jardine four-speed gear and all-chain drive, is a most desirable sidecar mount.

Above is a wonderful show machine, the opposite side of an earlier picture, minus its primary and rear chain covers. There is plenty of plating indicated. From as early as 1913 Campion on their show machines plated hubs and anything else, the result was fantastic. Thanks to TCM Publications.

1917 Brought innovation with ambulances and innovations with coal gas, dealt with in the Sidecar and Wartime Chapters. One such ambulance was donated to Birmingham City. There was a new J.A.P 4hp model fitted with a Sturmey-Archer 3-speed gearbox and a sidecar outfit fitted with hub greases. Stuart Speedos were fitted.

Oh Look It's AU133 yet again? TCM.

This was a new J.A.P 8hp engine with new lubrication and fins on the exhaust caps. It was fitted with Sturmey-Archer 3-speed counter shaft gearbox. The sidecar could carry one person as a hinged boot was incorporated for extra fuel, tools and luggage. The machine was 1 ½ inches higher than the norm.

1918 saw an abundance of second hand machinery on the market. Campion were still manufacturing aircraft parts, but offered upgrades and new models. The most important of which was a unit construction cycle and sidecar frame. I don't think this continued for long. Also offered was a new Villiers two-stroke lightweight, a J.A.P 4hp fitted with 28 x 3 inch wheels, and a new J.A.P 90-degree V-Twin, also fitted with 28-inch wheels.

Here is my 4hp with the 1918 J.A.P Engine and Sturmey-Archer 3-speed gearbox.

Here was my machine as I began making parts and doing a dry run assembly.

1919 had plenty of action in the Competition Chapter as Clubs got back to normal, and new faces appeared on the scene. Olympia covered limited choices of machines as would be expected. The only model commented on was the sidecar outfit. The opening comments are a lesson for most companies as well as Campion.

It read,

"The Campion is one of those machines which would be better known if the output of its manufacturers were larger!" The sidecar machine in question is described as larger than most, and a common sense unit built by "keen road men."

Campion produced as many as 45 machines a week. Not bad for what was considered as a small company!

Campion 5-6 h.p. sidecar outfit, fitted with three-speed gear and all-chain drive.

This model has a very strong rectangular duplex frame for the sidecar fitted with a step. The motorcycle has a larger capacity tank. Note the change in the front brake. Campion always used the stirrup bicycle brake on solo machines, however on combinations they used this brake, as it was stronger. This model had the front and rear wheels interchangeable. This was to be the last year for this system.

The picture above was used for three consecutive years to advertise the machine at shows, which gets very confusing, but this was the first and most important. It was the most talked of model of all of the Campion`s exhibited. Note the registration number till later? Thanks to TCM for the extract.

1920 saw Campion gaining credit for the First Taxi. Covered in the Sidecar Chapter. Campion in conjunction with a subsidiary company the Nottingham Motorcycle Taxi Company, set up on Byard Lane, Nottingham. They were producing taxis offering the luxurious two seaters also to motorists requiring the room for family transport at a price of £250. Interestingly fitted with a foot operated and hand operated 2 band on hub braking system.

There was also plenty of action in competition, which I believe was down to a new Blackburne 10hp engine. This does not seem to have become a production model until a few years later, but certainly made a serious impact on the racing scene.

This is an original picture kindly lent to me by John Beaty. It portrays Mr S.S. Debenham astride his winning 10hp Blackburn powered Campion that he won so many awards. The scene is the Trent Embankment, Nottingham about 1919/20. The Cup is the Campion Trophy. The passenger may be Alfred or Charles? What a machine! All Chain drive, interchangeable wheels. Two oils feed to either side of the engine. Mag/dymo. Druid Forks. Also a new saddle tank.

The Nottingham M.C.C presented him with a silver pocket watch engraved with the three wins in 1919, The Campion Cup, The Dennis Bayley Cup, and the Raleigh Cup. I need this bike? His daughters Nancy and Betty became pin ups for BSA in the twenty's.

A larger engine, the J.A.P 986cc 85 ½ x 85mm, fitted with an Amac and 3-speed Sturmey-Archer gearbox, all chain drive, was offered for sidecar and solo use.

1921 was again a good year for success in competition. I have covered as much as I can find to a Chapter of the same name. At Olympia an all-new frame for the motorcycle was designed giving uncluttered and cleaner lines. It was fitted with Campion's first saddle tank. Thanks to TCM Publications for this.

The Campion is a Nottingham representative of the big twin sports type.

What a Baby? This was classed as the Super Sports Model fitted with the 976cc J.A.P engine and Jardine 4 speed gearbox. Drum brakes all round, wheels that were interchangeable and offered in two touring models with 8-inch mudguards. We also see a new exhaust system.

Obviously with Campion, a choice of an everyday or luxurious sidecar is available also carrying a spare wheel. The style of the above is somewhat familiar?

Also on display was a 250cc Villiers model, with a sloping top tube. There was the introduction of the 348cc Blackburne powered model and a J.A.P of a similar size engine, and a separate oil tank was offered.

1922. Stand 72. Campion displayed seven machines, the most striking being the 976cc super sports and sidecar. It was very much similar as the previous year.

1923. Letters rather than hp now identified models together with minor additions. See lists at the rear of this Chapter.

Above and below are photographs of Alistair Brown's 650 J.A.P a fine running example.

Mr Beaty loaned me these original leaflets from 1922, indicating the 1923 models.

1924 brought a surprising new development at Olympia. On stand 15, Campion introduced the Blackburne 250 models, but more importantly the Aero Forks. Highly braced diamond shape in profile, fitted with top springs similar to Earl's. Pivoting from top spindle in the fork, and to the lower yoke and lower fork spindle so that movement between the fork and the cycle exerts oppositely directed forces on the springs. These were patented over a two-year period together with a Mr Harry Markham.

The Forks referred to as GB 19230018774 19230721 springs
GB 19240021047 19240906 forks

I can find no photographs of machines with these forks, other than drawings recorded in the patent records. I know models after this time reverted back to the druids, or was it simply cheaper?

The following year saw continued but lower production of models listed, often made to order. There is little innovation after this, but more of a wind down of production as demand became less.

A very nice post card of a 1925 Campion with a Blackburne Engine and pressed steel chain case. Note the tax disc holder on the bars, full leg shields and a teddy on the forks! This was acquired from a well-known auction site.

1925 still saw roads tests on sidecar models, but no new models. There were no new models in 1926 and 1927. In the latter year, Curry's had taken control of the companies shares but allowed limited production to continue, especially with the New Gerrard. There were plenty of second hand machines for sale at the main depots in Nottingham, together with a BSA range offered.

1928 saw only one advert for a new Campion, together with second hand machines of other makes. They were still retailing new bicycles but by now all was ending with the sale of the plant and machinery and then the main factory. The takeover was not completed till 1930. See Chapter relating to H. Curry.

The following is an easy reference list of years and developments, starting 1889.

1889. Fast Van. Consisted of a large box on a forecar, (see Bicycle Chapter), with smaller Campion engine. This developed into the 3.75hp forecar, which was water-cooled. Also the first motorcycle powered by own 2hp engine. The double-sided number plate began and continued as a feature on all machines till the end.

1901. Campion 3.75hp Forecar, water-cooled.
Minerva 2hp single.

1903. Minerva 3 ½ hp single.

1904. 2 ½ hp, 2 ¾ hp, 3 ½ hp Singles. The smaller motors were still there own engine shown here. A Vertical unit bolted within the frame. Difficult to make out specific details, but again it is the only photo I can find.

1905-10.

Campion 4hp water-cooled Forecar, 2 speeds, continued for only a few years.
Peugeot 3 ½ hp twins and a 5hp model, with an Armstrong 3 speed gearbox, 26 x2 wheels, and £45.
J.A.P 2 ½ hp and 4 hp with 2 speed Armstrong.
NSU twin (fitted from 1906-1911).

Thanks to
TCM
Publications

Minerva 4 ½ hp Fittall 2-speed gearbox.

1911. J.A.P 6hp twin and sidecar, all chain drive.

1912
Saw the introduction of the J.A.P 4hp model and Peugeot 3 ½ hp with Roc 2-speed gear hub. These models were already being built much earlier, but it was described as such due to their first appearance at a large show. Precision engines in 3 1/2hp sizes were also used.

Campion also supplied the following;
J.A.P 3 ½ hp with Armstrong gears.
Green or Villiers two strokes 2 ½ hp

1913

HP	No of Cylinder	Bore	Gear	Wheel Size	Price
2 ½	1	70 x 76	2 sp CcB CS	26 x 2 ¼	
4	1	85 ½ x 85	3 sp CcB CS	26 x 2 ½	61
6	2	76 x 85	3 sp CcB CS	26 x 3	73
8	2	85 ½ x 85	3 Sp CcB CS	26 x 3	75

1915

Additional 8hp model available with Jardine 4 speed gearbox. This was fitted or offered as an alternative through to 1925. Some machines were fitted with this in 1914.

Villiers

2 ½	1	70 x 70	2 sp CcB CS	26 x 2 ¼	34
2 ½	1	70 x 70	Fx	26 x 2 ¼	28

1918. The new druid forks were fitted.

1921

2 ½	1	70 x 70	2 sp SA chain/blt	26 x 2 ¼	65
4	1	85 ½ x 85	3 sp SA chain/blt	26 x 2 ½	100
6	2	76 x 85	3 sp SA chain	28 x 3	130
8	2	85 ½ x 85	3 sp SA chain	28 x 3	132

1922 as for 1921 with 1 additional model. Sidecars fitted varied between £20 and £40.

4	1	70 x 76	2 sp SA chain/blt	28 x 2 ¼	66

1923. Models are designated letters as model identification.

K.2 ½	1	70 x 70	2 sp SA chain/blt	26 x 2 ¼	50
J2 ¾	1	70 x 76	3sp SA chain	26 x 2 ¼	62
JB2 ¾	1	70 x 76	2sp SA chain/blt	26 x 2 ¼	58
G4 ½	1	85 ½ x 85	3sp SA chain	26 x 2 ½	85
F8	2	85 ½ x 85	3sp SA chain	28 x 3	100
D8	2	85 ½ x 85	3sp SA chain	28 x 3	110
S8	2	85 ½ x 85	4sp Jar chain	28 x 3	110

(Sports)   Sidecars fitted, depending on specification, were between £30 to £50 extra.

1924. Saw models again using the lettered prefix.

The models available were the above models J, F, D, which now had the new J.A.P drip feed and splash lubrication. Also there was a Villiers 175cc model.
The new Aero Forks were now available, fitted to sidecars. Also the smaller Blackburne engines were introduced as fitted to the New Gerrard, but I have found a few 249cc as early as 1921. They were launched at Olympia this year.

249cc Blackburne Sv or Sports ohv
348cc Blackburne Sv or Sports ohv

1925

Models followed on from 1924. There no more show appearances. 1926 saw fewer models available and New Gerrards being advertised, from Carlton Depot. This seems to be the last full production year. There seems to be a glut of various makes of second hand machinery with odd new Campion`s appearing in 1927, apparently made to order. Please see the Chapter relating to New Gerrard and possible continued production at Bathley St.

1929

Saw a battle of advertising between Campion at Pelham St, (now Curry`s) and E.W. Campion and Sons of Station St. The latter having a new BSA franchise. Both were still dealing with second hand Campion Motorcycles.

1930

Pelham St and Carlton Rd, were selling Campion Cycles together with Hercules, and BSA. Also gramophones, wireless, and kits. I refuse to comment? At least Campion`s were still around for sale into the mid 1930`s.

List of Shows Attended

1911 Leicester Show. Attended with H. Curry.
1912 Leicester Show.
1913 Olympia Show. Campion's first national event.
1914 Olympia Show.
1919 Olympia Show.
1920 Olympia Show.
1921 Olympia Show.
1922 Olympia Show.
1923 Olympia Show.
1924 Olympia Show.
1925 is listed on some sites but is incorrect.

Throughout the range of motorcycles, Brown and Barlow, Amac, and Binks (from 1917) carburettors were fitted.

Similarly, Bosch, BTH, EIC, Lucas, and Splitdorf, magnetos were utilised with dynamos.

CAMPION SIDECARS.

Campion built their own and fitted other manufactured sidecars with standard fittings from 1903. It was found that these were lacking in strength and stability. Campion were one of the first companies to ensure that a four-point fixing became standard.

Here we have AU 133 again! Sporting different forks, and heavily laden!

Thanks to Mr Beaty for this and TCM Publications for The Last Straw

THE LAST STRAW!
A 4-5 h.p. twin Campion outfit which conveyed the Southwell, Notts, Junior F.C., from dressing room to playing ground, a distance of half a mile, in one instalment. Total weight of passengers was 16 cwt. 2 qrs.

Sidecars were a serious affair, built to the highest standards in aluminium on an ash frame. They were upholstered in leather often to match the livery, with screens and hoods. The screen edges were bound in leather. They were mounted with C type springing, hidden from view, which gave more graceful lines. A spare wheel was carried in a case at the rear of the chair, on which luggage could be strapped. An Additional spare wheel could also be carried. Initially only one brake was fitted to the rear wheel.

This photograph was taken at Nottingham Castle. You can see the features of the wartime ambulance that was also utilised in outfits provided to the mining villages and other areas of industry. This picture was taken in 1916. Credits to Nottingham City Council and Picture the Past Organisation for this, and the aluminium sidecar photo. One ambulance example was donated to Birmingham City Council.

There were two patents GB 19240021047 referring to the ambulances although were about in 1917 and GB19190007667, which related to a sport all aluminium sidecar shown below.

The Taxi outfit was available to all people for all uses. Thanks to TCM

The Aluminium Sports Sidecar had the chassis incorporated within the fine body. There was also room for tools and extra fuel.

"Campion" Aluminium Sidecar

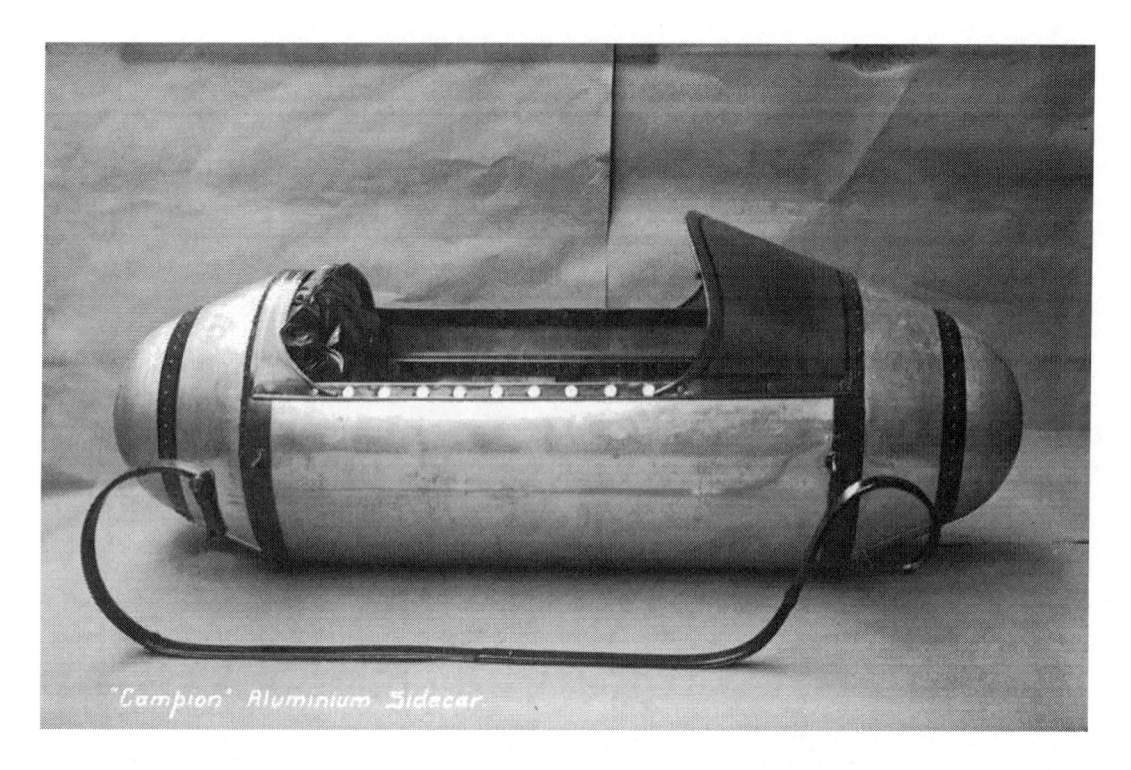

After the war wheels became interchangeable with an internal expanding 7¼ inch hub. What an unusual size? Also a Hand brake for parking was fitted. The all chain drive was covered with an aluminium chain case. All of which were useful on the first Motorcycle Taxis appearing in 1920. The trend continued up to 1928.

Taxis were sold around the country to Cities amidst the need to save fuel. Others were used as family transport. Campion takes the credit for the first taxi, which was always controversial in its use. It was even argued over in Parliament, but in 1920 Nottingham saw its first of many.

Nottingham Taxi Sidecars.

Sir,—I beg to inform you that on June 14th last my Watch Committee granted three licences for cycles and sidecars to ply for hire as taxi cycles, provided they were worked by ex-service men only. They are under the same regulations as for taxicabs.

The machines are 6 h.p. Campions, and the sidecars are built to carry two passengers.

The fares charged are 1s. for the first mile, and 8d. for each succeeding mile, with a proportion charge of 8d. for each succeeding proportionate part of a mile.

There is a taximeter fitted on the front of each sidecar in order that the passengers can read the distance they have travelled and the amount of fare due.

These cycles are giving every satisfaction to the public.

F. BROOK (LT.-COL.),
Chief Constable, Nottingham.

THE FIRST TAXI-SIDECAR.
The first taxi-sidecar to be officially passed by Scotland Yard. The body is of the two-seater type, and the machine a Campion.

This picture is dated 1920. The First Taxi, and is the same vehicle shown below.

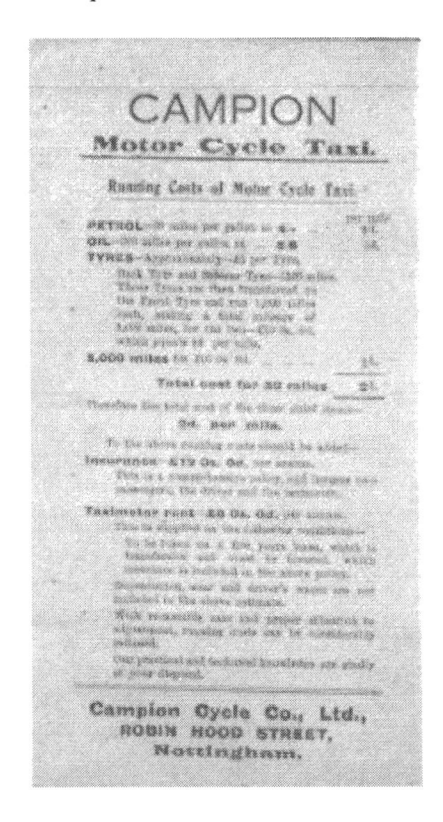

Left are the actual costings for running a taxi. Nottingham insisted the jobs went to ex servicemen. Thanks to Mr Beaty for this

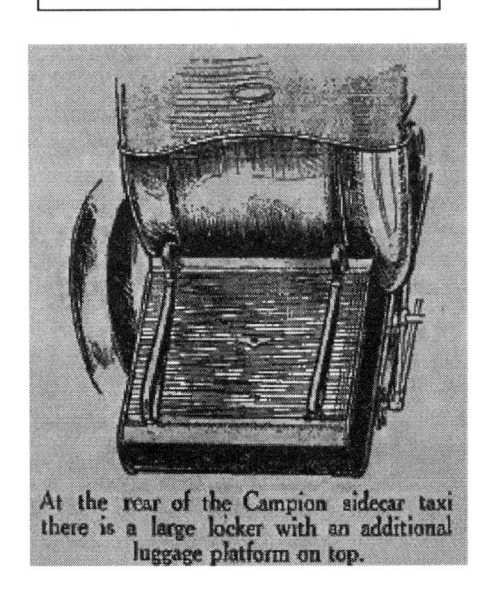

At the rear of the Campion sidecar taxi there is a large locker with an additional luggage platform on top.

Fantastic photo of the first Taxi in Nottingham dated 1920. The Registration Number is the same as seen in the above show illustration and earlier.

The quickest and most pleasant way from convalescence to fitness. Private Hugh Smith, A. and S. Highlanders, who was wounded at Neuve Chapelle, is now at home and enjoying runs on the Campion sidecar outfit shown above.

The sidecar at the time was a real utility vehicle for those who could not afford a car. Many ex-servicemen had them adapted because of loss of limbs. They were also supplied to the Red Cross, GPO (painted red for Sheffield), and the Police at Birmingham, Luton, Sheffield, and London. Thanks to TCM for the use of this advert.

As well as the Taxi, Nottingham was one of the first Counties to use them as Police vehicles. The argument was that the machines not only saved fuel, but they were also more mobile in town traffic. An argument brought to Parliament when the applications for taxis were put forward.

The Nottingham police authorities were among the first to recognise the value of the motor cycle in police work, and have for several years employed sidecar outfits. These two machines—a Campion and Raleigh, both made locally—are recent additions to the fleet.

The military was a good source of recruiting for most Police Forces. Here we have two gentlemen of that era. Wonder what is in the sidecar? TCM.

Here is a great picture of a genuine 1912 outfit. Not many about. She must be one of the most travelled having left the factory, finding her was to Australia and is currently in California, USA. Thank you to Waldema Osinski for the use of his picture.

Four generations of Williamsons, of Nottingham, on a Campion. The driver may be remembered by some of our readers as "Uncle Sturmey" of T.T. fame, the Sturmey-Archer gear expert, who died suddenly some time ago.

Along with Uncle Sturmey, other riders of combinations were John Jardine, and most of the Campion family. Thanks to TCM.

Certainly in competition, sidecars were put through their paces. Non-more than George Hunt's machine that ran for five years, also being subject to many road trials for competition. See Associations and Competition Chapters.

I have included this original photo of about 1917. I cannot say exactly who both of these gentlemen are. In the sidecar is Charles Campion. I thought the rider could be Captain Albert Ball, but not sure? He does sport a broken nose, however a great picture of a sporting outfit with pegs rather than footboards. Thanks to Mr Beaty for the loan of this.

CAMPION CARS

This chapter opens by discussing the interpretation of a car. In the early days a chair on the front of a bicycle, two wheels at the front, one wheel at the rear, and an engine in the middle was called a forecar. To confuse the issue, it was also called a motorised tricycle, as sometimes referred to by Campion. The exposure to passengers at the front to the elements soon brought the evolution of passenger carriages to be placed behind the front wheels, usually to carry two people, called a tricar. Four wheels soon came as standard, with a body in the style of the early 1900's horse carriages, referred to as quadcar or cycle car. This became streamlined to save weight and as long as it was under 772lbs (1912), it was classed as a heavy light car?

Motorcycle sidecars, were there to keep the true essence of the motorcycle. It enabled passengers to be carried safely, and was seen from around 1903 onwards. The light car became stronger and faster, with new chassis and larger more reliable engines up to 8hp, which drove you and your passenger around up to 20 mph. By 1914 they were achieving 45mph and some even more.

These were very popular with those who had money, but the industrial revolution brought about changes in social behaviour and the average person was able to afford a motorcycle, but not yet a car? There was an option available that was the next rung on the ladder called a light car. This was not everyone's idea of goodtime, for instance the lighting was bad, so one of the disadvantages was that not many ventured out at night. Petrol was sold at the chemist and very few outlets, but you have to understand that this was the beginning? One must not forget that light cars are still being built (Fiat 500 etc) and now we have the urge to use electricity as power. From the late 1800's electricity by way of batteries were already being used, so not a new idea. Coal gas was also used. Very soon after, larger cars to carry the family were being built, but they were expensive to build and to buy, so Campion remained with the light car. Campion, having built their own engines, were soon producing forecars and light vans from as early as 1899.

Early Advert from 1899. BNA.

What is a Quick Delivery Van I hear you ask? Before people were carried around for pleasure on machines, the original concept was to move goods in factories and from one factory to another. Initially by way of a tricycle with a box on the front (see Campion Bicycle Chapter). Followed by a powered version that had a wicker box basket to replace the box. Below is the very earliest example of a Campion forecar.

This photo was kindly loaned to me by John Beaty. It is the earliest Campion example of a forecar/tricar. Minimal fittings, no lights etc. Hand crank to start it on the variable pulley. Lighter Chassis rails than the later model. Water-cooled engine similar to that of the 1902 machine. These are the only pictures at present of the Campion engines. Radiator positioned in front of the handlebars. The brakes are the same as later models and so is the livery. Typical Campion leather tool bag on the seat. Elegant passenger seat, stolen from the green house? Fantastic rear brake! Joking apart, enjoy this? It is the only original photo, and dates this machine as early as 1900.

Charles Campion with his wife riding this forecar, dated 1902. The chassis rails are significantly strengthened. There is now a pedal start, and still on a variable pulley. Lights are now fitted, and a modern seat. Braking is the same as the earlier model, minus the brick? Thank you to Nottingham Historical Film Unit for this photograph and Picture the Past Organisation.

From 1903 Campion were building a light car, with their own engine. These engines were 2, 2 ¾, 3 and 4hp units. Often water-cooled. There are no examples about (yet?).

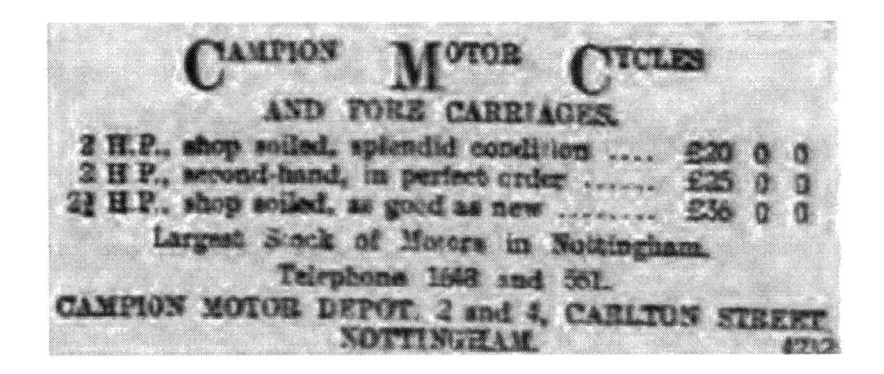

Advert from 1903. The 2 ¾ hp is a forecar. BNA.

The Campion power unit was dropped as early as 1904 in favour of proven units from other manufacturers. In the end it was all about sales and competitive retail prices. After all they had the facilities for chassis and coachwork, so adapting to build cars was not a problem.

THE CAMPION CYCLE CAR.

A neat cycle car is being marketed by the Campion Cycle Co. of Nottingham. The engine is an 8 h.p. J. A. P., the drive being transmitted through friction gear to a countershaft and thence by one inch belts to the rear wheels. Five speeds forward and one reverse are obtainable, and 650 x 65 tyres are fitted throughout. A Solex carburetter supplies the mixture.

George Campion in the Cycle Car. Note the use of the solex carburetter!
Thank you to the TCM Publications for the use of this picture.

By 1911 they were utilising the J.A.P engine in sizes of 6 and 8hp. Transmission wise, they remained with the belt drive to both rear wheels till 1920. Interestingly they sold a light car called the Richardson, during the 1920`s. I have found no details on this as yet.

The Above Campion light Car dated 1913 is powered by the J.A.P V-twin and is flanked by a Campion left (Charles) and Singer (Alfred) motorcycle. Thank you to The Nottinghamshire Historical Unit and Picture the Past Organisation for this.

Campion, experienced with developing these cars, also built chassis for The Dukeries Motor Company, located at Peck's Hill, Mansfield, Nottingham, up to 1920. The DMC Cyclecar as it was called, began about 1913. Again there are no examples, but please see the Chapter on Associates where I also refer to the DMC motorcycle.

CAMPION COMPETITION

What I have tried to do is list the known events and results in which Campion's are placed. There are shortcomings due to lack of information, but most are here. They are listed in date order, name of competitor machine, and placing.

1907.

Long Eaton and District M.C.C. Mr F. Cowlinson 4 ½ hp Campion/JAP. Third.
Shamrock M.C.C. Hill Climb. Mr James Miller 2 ¾ HP Campion. Third.

1908.

Nottingham M.C.C. Hill Climb at Bunny Hill. Amongst the entries were George Brough on a 3 ½ hp Brough, and Mr H. Jackson on a 7hp Campion/JAP. Neither was placed. ACME-Bentinck was placed first.

1911.

Lincolnshire A.C. Speed trial at Grimethorpe Park. Mr J. Harston on a Campion/JAP 4hp was placed second.

Nottingham and District M.C.C. Speed trial at Clipstone (Whitegates). Mr J. Harston on the Campion/JAP 4 hp was a heat winner, together with George Brough.

Derby and District M.C.C. Reliability trial. Mr J. Betts on a Campion/JAP 3 ½ hp with a Lyso belt, gained fourth place.

Lincolnshire M.C.C. Held a petrol consumption test. Mr J. Harston Campion/JAP 4hp Was the winner attaining 160mpg!

1912.

Lincolnshire A.C. Held a hill climb at Stanton Hill. Mr J. Harston Campion/JAP 4hp placed first.

Leicester and District M.C.C. Held a hill climb at Beacon Hill. Mr R.V. Wainwright Campion/Jap 3 ½ hp was awarded a Class 2 win.

Sheffield University M.C.C. Hill Climb. Mr R.B. Nicholson Campion/Jap 4hp. Class winner.

Sheffield and Hallamshire M.C.C. Held a hill climb near Baslow. Mr R.B. Nicholson, Campion/Jap 4hp gained a win in class 3.

The Motorcycle (newspaper), held their own National Team Trial. Each team having six entrants from each club. The Winning Team was Nottingham consisting of

Mr N.O. Soresby 3 ½ hp Rudge.
Mr J. Farnsworth. 3 ½ hp Rover.
Mr C.R. Smith 4 ½ hp CCR.
Mr J.R. Richards 3 ½ hp Sun.
Mr J.R. Sylvester 3 ½ hp Sun.
Mr A. E. Lole. 8hp Campion/Jap.

Wath and District M.C.C. Hill Climb at Bromborough. Mr. W. Nicholson Campion/JAP.

> Now that you have decided to have a motor-cycle do not be content with anything short of a
>
> **CAMPION**
>
> For speed, easy-running, and freedom from mechanical troubles, it has no equal
>
> **STILL WINNING**
> Mr. J. P. Nicholson, of Sheffield, on his Campion, did the fastest time and was First on Formula in the Wath and District Motor Cycle Hill Climb

The Campion/JAP 3 ½ hp was placed Second.

Thanks to the British Newspaper Archives.

Sheffield, Hallamshire and District M.C.C. Held a reliability trial to Holyhead and return. Covering 640 miles, there was an incredible four competitors tying for first place. Mr R. B Nicholson Campion/JAP 3 ½ hp was placed fourth.

Lincolnshire A.C. Held a speed trial. Mr J.E. Harston Campion/JAP was placed third in class 2.

A.C.U. 6-Day Trial. A large number of entries, including 2 Campions. Mr George

Brough won a Gold Medal. Mr G. Hunt Campion/JAP 3 ½ hp G & H gear, won a Silver Medal. Mr J. Farnsworth retired.

Merseyside M.C.C. An Open Trial was held. Mr G. Hunt Campion/JAP 3 ½ hp won a Gold Medal.

Belfast & Northern Ireland M.C.C. Held a100 mile reliability trial. Mr James Miller Campion/JAP 6 ½ hp. First place.

Leicester and District M.C.C. Held a hill climb. Mr W.R. Chapman Campion/JAP 6hp was placed first in class B.

Leicester and District M.C.C. Held a 56-mile road trial. Mr T. Nedham Campion/Jap 3 ½ hp was placed first.

Leicester and District M.C.C. Held a trial at Kettleby. Mr W.R. Chapman Campion/JAP 6 hp secured first place in the multi cylinder sidecar class.

Lincolnshire A.C. Held a petrol consumption trial. Mr J.E. Harston Campion/JAP 3 ½ hp secured second place.

1913.

Belfast and Northern Ireland M.C.C. Held a Hill Climb. Mr James Miller Campion/JAP 3 ½ hp won class two.

Nottingham and District M.C.C. Held a reliability trial in which there were solos and a team event for The Campion Cup. Mr Elborne, Triumph, won the Solo. Third was Mr Harold Marshall, Campion. The Team prize was won George Brough setting the fastest time of the day.

Leicester and District M.C.C. Held the Edwards Cup Trial. Mr R.G. Wainwright Campion/JAP 3 ½ hp was placed fourth.

Coventry M.C.C. Held an annual hill climb. Mr S. Briggs Campion/JAP 8hp was second in class five.

Glasgow M.C.C. Held a flexibility hill trial. Mr W. Turpin Campion/JAP 6hp South

Winners of the team prize in the Nottingham and District M.C.C. Reliability Trial for the Campion Cup. From left to right they are G. Brough, W. A. McKegzie, and T. Bigley, all of whom rode 6 h.p. Brough machines.

Great men on great machines. Love this picture. Full of atmosphere, you can sense the competition? Thanks to TCM Publications for the use of this.

Leicester and District M.C.C. Held a hill climb at Nevill Holt Hill. Mr R. Wainwright, Campion/Precision 3 ½ hp, was placed third in the open class and second in the handicapped class.

A.C.U. 6 Day Trial. Included over 160 entries. Mr G. Hunt Campion/JAP 3 ½ hp with an outstanding performance won a Silver Medal.

A Special Speed Trial was held at Gainsborough together with local clubs. Mr W.E. Waddington Campion/Precision 3 ½ hp was placed third in the general class.

Leicester M.C.C. held a 74 ½ mile Road Trial for the Quarterly Edwards Cup. Mr R. Wainwright, Campion was placed first.

Lincolnshire A.C. Held a reliability trial. Mr J.E. Harston Campion/JAP 6hp was placed second.

Lincolnshire A.C. Held a hill climb at Bunkass Hill. Mr E. Kemp Campion/JAP 4 ½ hp came third in class two. Mr J.E. Harston Campion/JAP 6hp gained a first place in class three.

W. E. Waddington, the active president of the North Derbyshire Motor Cycle Club. He rides a 3½ h.p. Campion-Precision, and enjoys competition work.

Great picture of Mr Waddington together with his machine. He was a member of the North Derbyshire Club. TCM publication

1914

South Wales Automobile Club and Cardiff M.C.C. Held a speed trials on the sands on a wonderful fine weathered day. It still took a few hours for the sands to dry out before competition commenced. Mr S.B. Briggs Campion/JAP 8hp was the fastest time of the day to secure first in the 'Up to 1000cc' class and the sidecar event.

Mersey M.C.C. Held the annual speed trial at Colwyn Bay. There was a good turn out for the event. Mr S.B. Briggs Campion/JAP 8hp won both the sidecar and up to 1000cc classes. His machine was remarked upon due to its fine plated finish, belt driven.

Grimsby and District M.C.C. Held a hill climb. Mr H.S. Jennison Campion won his class, as did Mr I. Rools Campion/JAP 6hp sidecar.

International Six Day Trial. Mr George Hunt Campion/JAP 8hp won a Gold Medal having the fastest time of the day. He was using for the first time the Jardine 4 speed gearbox.

Mr George Hunt aboard the trusty Campion/JAP 8hp with Jardine Gearbox. Note the twin headlamps, and wide mudguards. TCM.

The Streatham Club. Held a hill climb in very "slippy" conditions. Mr S.B. Briggs Campion/JAP won class ten and was second in the sidecar event.

Cicuito dell`Appenino Toscano. Held in Italy over 107 ½ miles, the fastest time of the day was by Mr S.B. Briggs, Campion/JAP 8hp.

Coventry and Warwickshire M.C.C. Held a hill climb. Mr S.B. Briggs Campion/JAP 8hp gained second place on his all plated machine.

Leicester and District M.C.C. Held a hill climb at Beacon Hill. Mr S.B. Briggs Campion/JAP 5-6 hp gained a first in solo and a first on the Campion/JAP 8hp sidecar.

Lincoln and District M.C.C. Held a Speed trial on the Mablethorpe sands. Mr S.B. Briggs Campion/JAP 5-6 hp won a first in the TT class and won the Sidecar class 4.

This wonderful picture of the Ladies event at Mablethorpe Sands. I had to include it. Left is Mrs K. Simpson (Rudge). Winner Miss Kettle (Premier). Right is Miss Shipside (Premier), aged only 16 yrs. Thanks to TCM Publications.

It is a shame these competitions cannot be re run? I appreciate the health and safety issues but one can dream? They were run in pairs, and first past the post winners. The Picture below is of Mr Briggs racing against a V-Twin Indian. Must have been fun to see?

Briggs on the Mablethorpe sands leading the Indian. Here is the plated machine he won so many awards thereon. TCM.

1915.

Mr G. Hunt Campion/JAP 8hp, Jardine 4 speed box, set the 24-hour Speed Record, covering 400 miles in 24 hours.

1916.

Mr G. Hunt Campion/JAP 8hp competed and did well in friendly trials at Matlock.

Interesting section of the Matlock trial. Mr Hunt on this run had issues with the spectators at the top! He cleared the section. Others found the flagstones slippery. TCM.

1919

Northampton M.C.C. Held a hill climb on Doddington Hill. Mr J. Brown Campion 2 ½ hp finished ninth.

Nottinghamshire M.C.C. Held the Dennis Bayley Challenge Cup. Mr S.S. Debenham Campion 10hp, won the Gold Medal.

Ilkeston and District M.C.C. Held a sixty-five-minute non-stop trial. Mr G.A. Calder Campion/JAP 4 ½ hp won a gold medal.

1920

The Reliance Cup Trials. This was held at Bwich-y-Groes, under extreme weather conditions. Mr P.K. Glazebrook, Campion/JAP 3 ½ hp was awarded a silver medal.

Dublin and District M.C.C. Held a trial in which Miss J. Moppett, Campion/JAP 6hp, Received a bronze medal, and Mr R.G. Winn, Campion was described as riding extremely well.

Campion was also doing well in New Zealand.

1921

Scottish Six-Day Trial. Having competed in where his stand dragged continually in one section, Mr J. Shepherd, Campion/JAP 6 hp, was awarded a Gold Medal.

Mr G Hunt and his trusty sidecar roaring up Picture Hill. I cannot find the name of the passenger during his racing career? TCM Publications.

Still Another Success.

GOLD MEDAL

FOR THE

CAMPION

IN THE

A.C.U. 6 DAYS TRIAL

Motor cycle and sidecar class (concluded July 11th), the highest award

GOLD MEDAL

was won by the all-conquering

CAMPION

ONLY ONE CAMPION ENTERED AND SECURED GOLD MEDAL.

However much more you may pay (and you can pay considerably more), you cannot get a more reliable motor cycle than the CAMPION, which is made in a model factory, by the most skilful mechanics in the trade.

Campion Motor Works
NOTTINGHAM.

Leicester M.C.C. Held a Two-Stroke Trial that was dominated by Velocette. Mr H. Ward, Campion won an award for the events pluckiest performer.

The London Exeter Christmas Trial. Over 182 motorcyclists competed in this Road Trial. Mr S.S. Debenham Campion 10hp was awarded a Gold Medal.

> CAMPION J.A.P. Racing Combination, 10-h.p., o.h.v., 4-speed, k.s., fine appearance and condition, winner of many prizes and trophies, £150.—Hollingworth, Widmerpool Station, Notts. 19445a

A rare advert for a sports machine. Could this be a Debenham machine? BNA.

LONDON — EXETER and back again.

A Jardine FOUR-SPEED GEAR was fitted to S. S. Debenham's 10 h.p. Campion Sidecar outfit, which completed the double journey without trouble and gained a **Gold Medal.**

YOU can depend on equal reliability when YOUR machine is fitted with a *Jardine Four-Speed Gear.*

Catalogues and Particulars from—
JOHN JARDINE, Ltd., Deering St., NOTTINGHAM.

> The Campion 10hp machine sported the Jardine gearbox. This set up was mainly used in the sports machines and was proved very reliable. TCM.

1922

Nottingham and District M.C.C. Held a Special Night Trial. Mr S.S Debenham Campion 10hp, received a special award.

Dublin and District M.C.C. Held a St Patrick's day reliability trial. Mr F.J. McMullen Campion/JAP 6hp. completed the course.

East Midland Centre A.A.U. Held an open trial in Derbyshire. Mr J. Cohen Campion 10hp, won an award.

Nottinghamshire M.C.C. Held a night trial covering some 144 miles. Mr S.S. Debenham Campion 2 ¾ hp, and Mr I. Cohen, Campion 10hp sidecar, were both awarded first.

London to Edinburgh. Mr S.S. Debenham Campion 10hp was awarded a Gold Medal.

Nottingham and District M.C.C. Held The Dennis Hayley Challenge Cup Reliability Trial. Held over 100 miles of Roads Mr J Cohen Campion was awarded a second place. Mr S.S. Debenham Campion was awarded a fourth position.

The Scottish Team Trial. Mr J. Cunningham Campion 976cc did well competing in the non-stops.

Nottinghamshire M.C.C. Held the East Midlands Trial for The Campion Cup. Mr I. Cohen Campion Sidecar won the cup.

The Campion Challenge Trophy, The Raleigh Challenge Trophy, and an unknown Trophy, (possibly the Dennis Bayley?) Where are they now? Mr S.S. Debenham won all three in one season and I wonder if this photograph was taken then? Thank you Mr Beaty for the use of this.

CAMPION WARTIME

No one expected the economic disaster that a world war brought to the lives of every day people and local businesses. Campion were no exception. How were they to plan ahead for next year and then the years ahead? No one had been in this situation before.

So what did Campion do? Production up to 1914 was very busy, with bicycles cars and motorcycles. However, after the first six months of war, people were not buying these machines or any others. In fact, people were selling their own machines as they went to war.

Thanks to TCM for the use of this advert.

Stock was building up, and retail prices were falling. The depots were not selling simply as there was no one to sell to? The most obvious customer for a motorcycle was a young man, but these were all going to war. All businesses at this time had to make drastic decisions to stay alive. Some stopped production completely, that is some companies mothballed everything. What a decision to make? To do this financially, you still needed equity to keep the factory, and machinery but lost skilled labour. Everyone found themselves in the same position, and all were losing their labour force.

In Nottingham was the MOD factory on Queens Drive, and also the depot at Chilwell. One of my early childhood experiences was visiting the Chilwell Depot with my father where you could bid at auction for groups of similar machines or parts wrapped in the brown paper and grease. My mother always ranted on our return either about what we came back with or the state we were in! Once we turned up with a trailer? Say no more.

One of the most secure options was to acquire a Ministry of Defence contract. These were offered to many industrial companies so they kept the labour force and produced ministry products for the war effort. This helped them stay in business. Campion were lucky in this case. They acquired a Ministry contract for aircraft parts. Such contracts were hard to get and jealously guarded. It affected Campion in a number of ways.

You have to relate to the period, where men went to work and women stayed at home to look after the house and the children. Campion boasted of the fact that no females were involved at the factories to compromise the quality of their machines. They stated this in many adverts. All this was about to change and thankfully never to return to this situation, although it still took many years to establish equality of the sexes with regards to skills and pay. An argument that still continues today.

To fulfil the MOD contracts, women were brought into the work place for the first time, working on production lines, they learned to use hand tools and machinery.

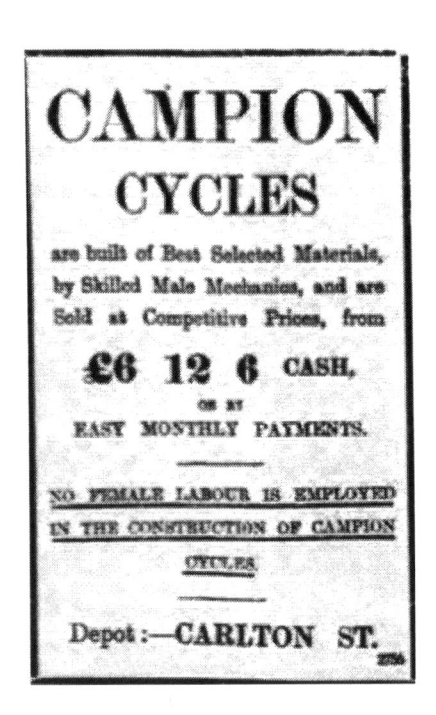

Women were also working on production lines. Above is an example of the advertising. The second photograph is of a lady working on a lathe at the Campion factory. Thanks to BNA and John Beaty. These adverts were never seen again.

What people did not realise is that Campion still produced motorcycles through out the war, but in lesser numbers. They were also able to develop new ideas into the motorcycles as advertised each year during the war, such as the four-speed Jardine gearbox. Sidecar outfits were built 1 and 1/2 inches higher from the ground, being more suitable for off road use. Many were exported to New Zealand. Machines in 1916 were painted Khaki as standard.

There was not the demand for new machines. Every other producer faced the same issue. No one knew when the war would end and propaganda made it even more difficult to survive. I don't know how they did it, as Banks were even more ruthless than now. There was a flood of second hand machinery, and to top it all prices were lower. Conscription affected every company, and every family. At this time, I had both of my grandfathers in France, and two Great Uncles. Albert emigrated to Australia, only to get called up in 1915 to go to Gallipolis. Having survived that he was only to die in France. RIP.

The effect on Campion's skilled labour was devastating. Although Campion tried to save employees jobs, training people as mechanics or to work in assembly lines, took time. After all, this industry was still in its infancy. This is most easily explained by comparison of the two original photographs of 1914 and 1918.

One such fatality of the war was a Private John Harry Spence, of The Sherwood Foresters who died from wounds 23/1/17 who worked at the Campion Factory.

In the latter picture you do not see the young gentleman as in the previous, although there are a few familiar faces.

This was typical of most industries of the period, and a sad loss to all. Thanks to John Beaty for providing these original photographs. The two gentlemen stood to the left, are Mr Ernest Hutchinson and George Campion.

The loss of skilled labour still affected Campion after the war, along with difficulty acquiring raw materials, and then being faced with the recession.

The above is a great photo of George and the ladies hard at work on aluminium aircraft parts in 1917. This photo, along with the two above, are taken at the Robin Hood Street Factory. The above was supplied by Nottingham City Council and Picture the Past.

A Camping scene with despatch riders from the Leicestershire Yeomanry. On the left a BSA, Douglas, Matchless, and Humber. Right, a Campion. Thanks to TCM.

Campion were adapting to the situation, but there was an interesting development regarding the contract of making the aircraft parts. These required aluminium welding, and for this you needed gas. No big deal now days, but then it was delivered by train to Station Street, where it was collected by Campion and taken to Robin Hood Street. Simply you would say? No, in reality it was not.

The fuel allowances were virtually nil for private use (gallon a week), and was not much better for companies. The Ministry provided the gas bottles, but Campion found that the fuel allowance did not stretch to cover the runs. So what did they do? Here we have the perfect solution?

Motorcycles adapted to run on coal gas with large balloons attached to the machine above the rider. The machines were strengthened to carry the cylinders.

There was a trap door beneath the balloon, which opened to equalise pressure. Surprisingly the V-Twin did not overheat, and ran well providing a little less to the gallon, but still did the job. The Gas bottles incidentally were carried on a strengthened sidecar. As you can imagine there was an awful amount of experimentation?

Campion did produce kits as well as other companies to attach to your car or motorcycle during the war. They worked well, however they naturally died off after 1918. That did not mean that these were never seen again. WW2 brought similar restrictions on fuel, and the balloons made another appearance.

Thanks to TCM Publications for this extract, also below in this chapter.

Part of a batch of prospective despatch riders passed by the Editor of *The Motor Cycle* on the 23rd ult. for the Royal Engineers Signal Service. They were tested on their own machines in the Coventry Barracks yard.

WAR. Second-hand Motor Cycles and Sidecars left by Volunteers gone to the front, extraordinary low prices to clear; example, 5-6 twin speed gear, free engine, and sidecar, £17 10s.—Campion, Carlton-street, Nottingham.

During the war competition was put on hold, although there were a few local activities to keep your hand in and to keep spirits up? The National Motorcycle Union had put an end to national competition, but asked for experienced motor bicyclists to join up as despatch riders to aid in telecommunications at home and abroad. Lots of riders joined up taking their own machines with them in some cases. At regular intervals, The Motorcycle provided details of such men and their experiences, and sadly their deaths. During this time, it is important to realise that technology in communication was at a very early point of development. Field radios were connected by wires covering often miles of dangerous territory and were often blown apart. It was the job of the despatch rider not only to deliver important messages but also to help repair these lines. It was crucial for a good rider to be kept going on a good machine. In the chapter regarding Innovation, you will see George Campion with a wireless set attached to the rear of his machine. The Future?

Campion Motorcycles although never mentioned in other publications, did take part in the Great War, and were used in local regiments.

Lincoln Yeomanry. Left Matchless, Ivy/Precision Campion/Jap Zenith.

In 1917, George Campion designed developed and patented the ambulance sidecars. Injured men were often stacked on vehicles and transported to safety. So was the need. In Campion's experience if there severely injured patients, they should be carried in relative comfort and protection, hence his design that allowed two stretches to be carried in one sidecar.

This was done by adapting the sidecar much to look like a bunk bed, with a cover and ample room to insert the two stretches. One of the two could also be carried in the seated position. Drain holes were in the bottom so they could be cleaned easily.

Described in more detail in Sidecar, and Models Chapters. The Ambulance carried two Stretches, had interchangeable wheels and a spare tucked in the rear.

A RED CROSS 8 H.P. AMBULANCE OUTFIT.
This unique sidecar is a recent production of Messrs. The Campion Cycle Co., Ltd., Nottingham, and permits the patient to lie flat or sit in a normal position. A semi-circular celluloid screen is fitted, which, with the hood, affords complete protection from the weather. The stretcher can be withdrawn from the rear of the sidecar.

The end of the war did not end business difficulties. Many smaller companies were never to be heard of again, others stayed alive with merges or takeovers. What faced everyone now was the recession.

There was still a lack of money, and a glut of second hand machinery on the market. Raw materials for production were very hard to come by and were expensive. Often it was only provided in limited quantities, which had a roll on effect with production.

Machines stood waiting for the importation of magnetos and tyres. Sadly, the other factor was the larger the company was, the more people you employed, the more materials were made available! This did not help small concerns. Many companies were never to be seen again. Interestingly many companies fitted German wheel rims, including Campion.

Below is a picture of the sale of 200 army bikes. The makes listed here were not standard Government machines, such as Triumph, or Douglas. There are a few surprises, but at the end of the day this was a pure availability decision. So for the first time, check these out. One may be yours?

Scott, Humber, Lea Francis, Indian, Matchless, Chater-Lee, Ariel, NUT, New Hudson, LMC, Grifton, Rex, Calthorpe, NSU, Motosocoche, BAT, James, Premier, Rover, Rudge, AJS, Campion, Regal, Excelsior, Royal Enfield, Singer, Bradbury, Zenith.

Sad to see them ending up like this, but surprisingly most of these were sold.
Prices were commented on as being quite high, but one assumes that these were bought by dealers and used either as spares or made good to sell as a cheap machine.

One of the heroes of Nottingham and of our Country during the WW1, is Captain Albert Ball VC. I could devote a whole Chapter to him. A man of Speed his chosen ride was a Campion.

Here he is on his trusty Campion V-Twin side valve 6hp of about 1916. The rear pulley gives an indication of quite a high-speed machine.

Albert Ball, born in Lenton, Nottingham, 14/8/96, is the equivalent of Brough`s Sir Lawrence of Arabia. For those of you who have never heard of our Nottingham hero, this young man was England's most feared fighter Ace of WW1, credited with 44 victories. He was awarded the VC, DSO, 2 BARS, MC, Legion D`Honneur (France), Order of St George (Russia), and Freeman of the City. Most important of all he rode a Vee Twin Campion!

A Close up to view the Campion name. This was confused with a Harley Davidson for years.

Capt Ball as early as 1915 became a lieutenant of the NMDCC? Yes, I thought that? It means the North Midland Divisional Cyclist Company. This was where dispatch riders were trained. Charles Campion also joined this unit at some point. From here Albert paid for his own flying lessons, and subsequently joined The Royal Flying Corps. Described as very much a loner, he developed a fearless style of flying in combat, and sadly met his fate crashing in low cloud 7/5/17.

Thanks to John Beaty for another original photograph.

Charles Campion aboard a V-Twin machine of about 1917. He wears the same uniform of Albert Balls NMDCC unit. AU133 appears in various locations in the book, or is it a trade plate? The rider and the bike should be 1917 but the forks confuse the issue. If you note the angular shape of these forks these are comparable with those fitted and patented in 1924. Confusing to say the least, and I have no answer to these appearing at this time on what is clearly a period photograph.

On the death of Capt Albert Ball, his foe showed considerable respect at his funeral. During his flying career, in particular his combat capabilities, which were known to be fearless, were successfully adopted into the fore coming training manual. It is said that after returning from combat, his plane was often refuelled in which he took of by himself in search of balloons etc.

There is a statue at Nottingham Castle of this famous pilot, and contributions in the museum.

R.I.P.

A True Campionite.

CAMPION ASSOCIATIONS

Mr Charles Binks, formerly from near Liverpool, after a partnership and then getting married in York, he settled in Nottingham. He conducted business at Aspley Engineering Works, Bobbers Mill Nottingham. He was building Bicycles here from 1900. A very talented engineer who built bicycles that was lighter than everyone else's. He developed his own brakes and other attachments that were exhibited at local and national events. A move to Wollaton St, into the Whitehall's factory in 1902, saw the production of lightweight and four-cylinder luxury motorcycles. The motorcycles were given a different name. They were referred to as The Evart Hall. Fitted to a diamond frame, the four in line 5hp engine had all chain drive, and aluminium enclosed cases. These were retailed from Goldsmith Street, Nottingham.

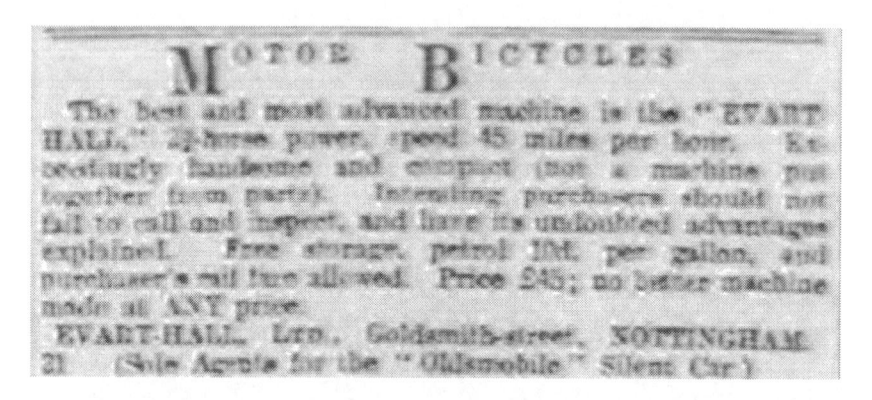

Cars of a similar calibre soon followed, for which he is wider known. They survived a dramatic fire in 1905, and continued production of multi cylinder cars. Due to the expense in production and no doubt the recession, Binks moved into something smaller to produce. Thanks to the British Newspaper Archives for the above. Together with his son Harold, they began manufacturing Carburettors simply known as the Binks. These were fitted to larger capacity machines to enhance performance. The earliest I have found is 1917. Charles died in 1922, his son continued.

Come the late 1920's the company was swallowed up within the take over of Almac to be within the Amal group. Mr H. Binks remaining a director till the 1950's.

Mr E. Chandler, at Peck's Hill, Mansfield, Nottingham, formed the Dukeries Motor Company Ltd, just before the Great War. It featured cyclecars built with their own 4 ½ and 8hp engines. Campion produced the chassis for these cars, which were built in their hundreds each year but declined in production to less than 100 by 1918. The 8hp engine was put into a motorcycle. Mr Chandler did compete on such a machine but the motorcycle at that time carried no name, and was place in a "Special" Class on its own. After, he named it the DMC, and received awards locally.

This is a Campion frame and running gear, with Chandler's own Engine. Note the Binks Carb as early as 1917. Thanks to TCM.

A SKILLED ENGINEER'S HANDIWORK.
This motor cycle, including the engine, was made entirely by Mr. E. Chandler, of the Dukeries Motor Co., Mansfield, in 1917. The specification includes a 7-9 h.p. twin engine, 83 x 97 mm., with side-by-side valves, Binks carburetter, U.H. magneto, and a four-speed gear box. Altogether the machine appears to be a well made and very sporting mount.

Mr George Hunt. A competitive cyclist in his day, that was to continue with Campion Motorcycles up to 1918. He won many events, and set records mainly with the sidecar outfit. He also had a cycle retail business, which sold parts and accessories, on Grey Friar Gate, Nottingham, known as The George Hunt Cycle Corporation.

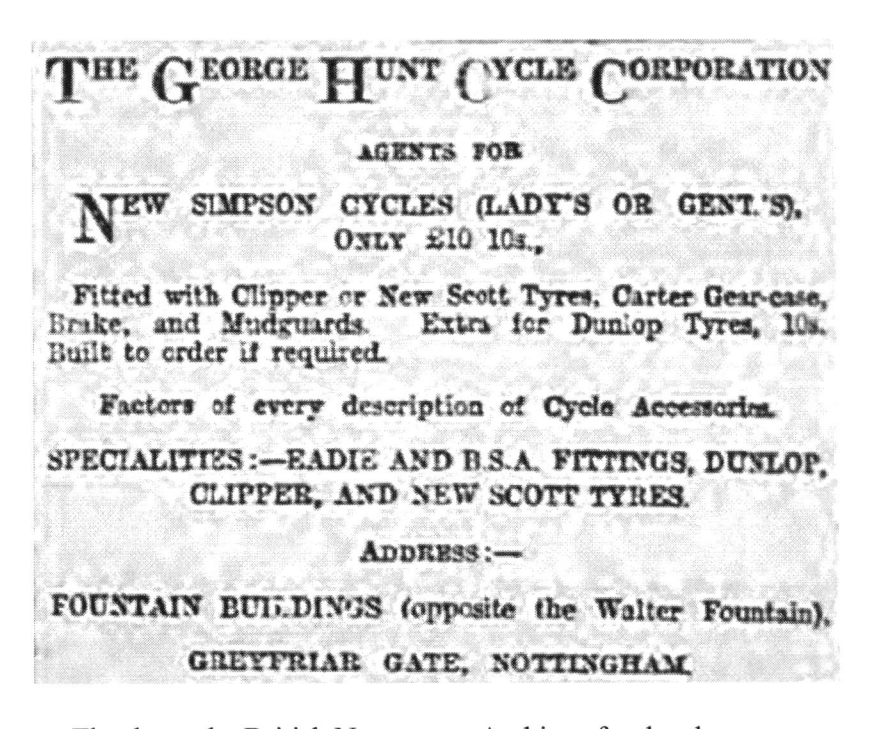

THE GEORGE HUNT CYCLE CORPORATION

AGENTS FOR

NEW SIMPSON CYCLES (LADY'S OR GENT.'S),
ONLY £10 10s.,

Fitted with Clipper or New Scott Tyres, Carter Gear-case, Brake, and Mudguards. Extra for Dunlop Tyres, 10s. Built to order if required.

Factors of every description of Cycle Accessories.

SPECIALITIES:—EADIE AND B.S.A. FITTINGS, DUNLOP, CLIPPER, AND NEW SCOTT TYRES.

ADDRESS:—

FOUNTAIN BUILDINGS (opposite the Walter Fountain),
GREYFRIAR GATE, NOTTINGHAM.

Thanks to the British Newspaper Archives for the above.

George Hunt on the new four-speed 8 h.p. Campion. Mr. Hunt, it may be mentioned, is the holder of the 24 hours cycle paced record, having covered over 400 miles in 24 hours.

In the 1920's he had set up with Charles Campion at Milton Works, Milton Street Nottingham, where they together ran a successful textiles mill but also designed and build machinery having numerous patents to their accreditation, from 1917 to 1924, to include two French patents, all relating to textile machinery. Thanks to TCM.

Mr Ernest Frederick Hutchinson ran his fathers lace factory on Russel St, Nottingham, which produced surgical hosiery. Another keen cyclist in his day, and president of the Nottingham Bicycle Club, he is recorded in 1888 (Wrights) as also being a cycle manufacturer, based at 37 Pelham St, Nottingham, together with Edwin Campion.

This is very interesting from the Campion prospective, as Edwin who worked with his father also had a separate concern with Mr Hutchinson, who in 1897 became one of the Directors of the Campion Cycle Company Ltd with Edwin. He was actively involved with the company until the Curry's take over was complete in 1930. During this he appeared to be the spokes person for Campion. He sadly died aged only 57 during 1929.

In 1923, the partnership of himself and Edwin as the Campion Factoring Company was dissolved. He also suffered a serious accident in his Humber car, from which he never fully recovered. The Campion Cycle Company Ltd, still continued, however I feel that this split up did cause friction with Edwin, who in 1925 took on other premises in Grantham, as E.W. Campion and Sons to following his own interests. Various outlets between the two were split equally, however 37 Pelham St, was still used by the Campion Company well into the 1930`s.

Left is Mr Hutchinson together with George Campion from the factory photo dated 1919

Mr Hutchinson drove a Humber in which he had a serious accident in 1912, and he rode a Campion Sidecar outfit. He resided at 1 Melton Rd, West Bridgford, and had one daughter.

Mr John Jardine, son of Ernest Jardine, inherited four lace factories, three in Nottingham, and one in Draycott, Derbyshire. The largest factory by far was Deering St, employing over 2000 people. On site he had his own foundry, and for years had been designing and making parts for textile machines. It was therefore ideal for making transmissions for which John later became known. He set up The Universal Motor Company in 1900, which included many variants of motorisation.

Thanks to BNA for this contribution

He never produced his own machines, but developed 2, 3, and 4 speed gearboxes that were fitted to various machines into the 1920's. These were reliable and sturdy units. There only failing was replacing parts as it was difficult to remove inners easily. He did build a 350cc unit construction engine and gearbox, but I can find nothing more about it.

The gearboxes began about 1912 with light versions, accumulating in the 4-speed box in 1914. Funnily enough the 3-speed did not arrive till shortly after the four-speed? I have covered the gearboxes in more detail within the chapter relating to Campion models.

New Gerrard. Jock Porter an engineer in Edinburgh built his own machines and bravely competed in the TT in 1922. Having retired, he came back in 1923 to win the 250cc class, again in 1923 on a 175cc, and in 1924 a third place again on the 175cc.

His success brought in business with demands for road machines, a proposition he could not deal with. He could not find experienced labour locally, so turned to Campion just down the Road. A deal was struck, and Campions, renamed New Gerrard was sent up by rail. This allowed Jock to continue with special order machines, as he preferred to work by himself.

Porter's Motor Mart also sold other second hand machines. In 1924 He used a Blackburne engine of 249cc or 350cc, sv or ohv. In 1926 there was 348cc model only, but also the more powerful sidecar unit the 549cc. In 1929 models declined to only the 348ohv engine, which was swapped to a J.A.P in 1930.

It is at this point that again Campion raises its head. Edwin Campion had moved to Station St, and Bathley St, Nottingham. These premises were active just after the Curry's take over in 1929. The production manager from Campion was brought to Station St. It is interesting to see that at Bathley St, it is recorded that E.W. Campion and Sons, were listed as motorcycle manufacturers. During the 1970's another Company continued the name and produced fibreglass fairings from there, well into the 1980's. Importantly when the premises was cleared, in the cellar was found amongst other things a cart belonging to George Campion, but more importantly a large quantity of motorcycle parts including headlights and other fitting. Is it likely or possible the New Gerrard was continued from Bathley St? After all, Edwin Campion acquired the tooling. The same Blackburne engines also powered the Campion models at the relevant times. Production of the New Gerrard was continued through to 1939, when Bathley St, was still active under Edwin Campion?

Mr Newton Wilson, I have covered in both the Bicycle and Textile Chapters. He was considered one of the most flamboyant figures of the Textile Industry and his contribution to it as creating the most sought after collectable machines in the world. His involvement in Bicycles likewise was a great contribution to production and development of the same, but his demise in the 1890's makes one wonder what he would have achieved once he had seen the early engines powering bicycles?

Mr Edward George Young always had a passion for cycling. As early as 1885 he is recorded as racing a tandem with Charles Campion. At the same time his first success was the Flying Triplet (tricycle). He was a founder of the Castle Bicycle Club, and was one of the founders of the Nottingham Motorcycle Club.

> Mr Young in his "Younger" Days was a very keen and fit cyclist. This does not surprise me in the least. BNA

About 1893, Mr Young became a manager for William Campion, at the London Rd factory. I am sure it is here that he was able to develop his skills in manufacturing techniques of bicycles that lead to his own make, and motorcycles and cars. At the factory at this time were not only bicycle manufacturing but also tyre sales and repairs. In 1885, William Campion moved production to Roden St, and left Mr Young to retail Campion products. It was not long until he was retailing his own make of bicycles and motorcycles and forecars.

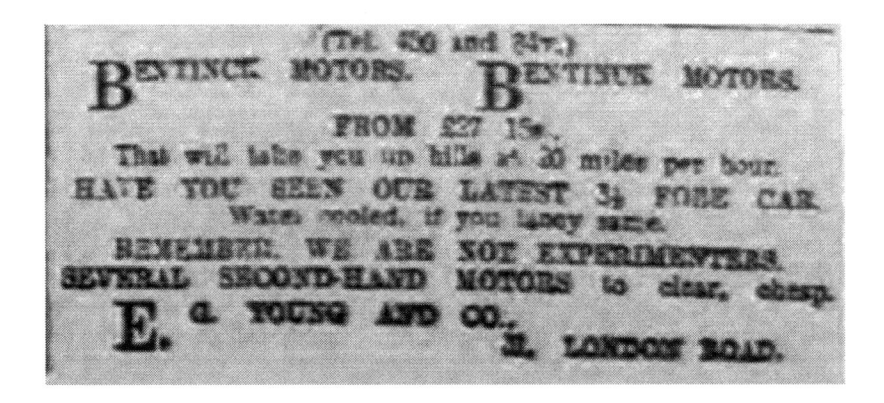

> Advert from 1903 BNA

Mr Young sold vehicles to order, called the "Bentinck" and took on a partner named Mr Bailey. The partnership only lasted two years, and then Young referred to the business as E.G. Young and Co. A very competitive man, he was soon boasting his own success with the bicycles that won local events, setting record times. The first motorcycle appeared in 1903, being a bicycle with an under slung Minerva Engine.

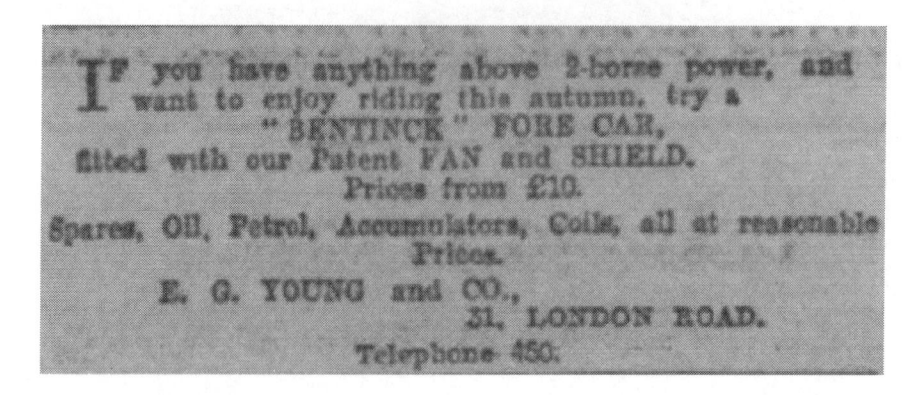

> IF you have anything above 2-horse power, and want to enjoy riding this autumn, try a
> "BENTINCK" FORE CAR,
> fitted with our Patent FAN and SHIELD.
> Prices from £10.
> Spares, Oil, Petrol, Accumulators, Coils, all at reasonable Prices.
> E. G. YOUNG and CO.,
> 31, LONDON ROAD.
> Telephone 450.

The fan assisted cooling was a patented idea in 1904, using a Minerva water-cooled single. Thanks to the British Newspaper Archives for the above. His own machines developed along similar lines as the period, with engine fastened vertically within the diamond frame, but again he was competitive, having two machines compete in the Tourist Trophy (Isle of Man), and competing generally with some success even beating George Brough in a local club event. Other power units were used including.

There was some involvement with ACME from 1907/8. ACME produced Minerva powered motorcycles, and there own 3hp engine. They were based in Coventry. It is recorded that they had two machines taking part in the 1908 TT, but retired. Interestingly a report says that two Bentinck machines did the same, so were these a joint venture? Was the picture below a Bentinck Frame with the ACME engine? I think this is more likely, as Bentinck machines are listed as competing in other events.

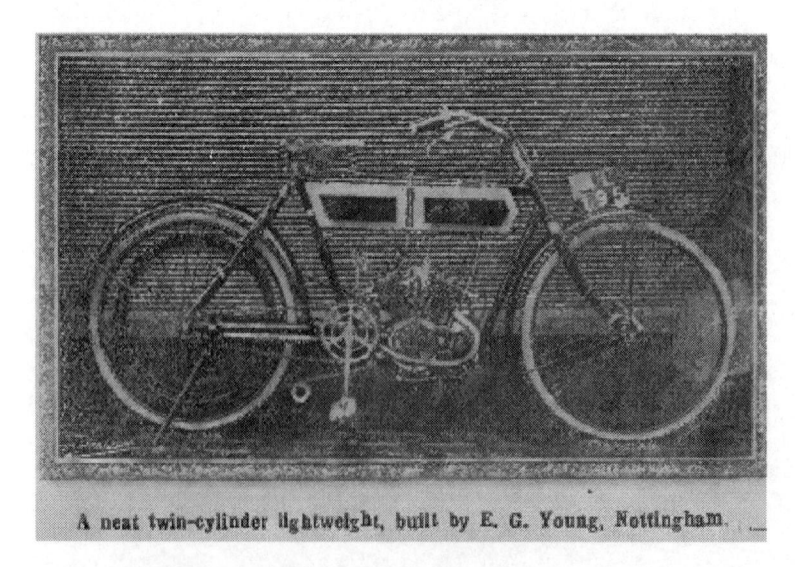

A neat twin-cylinder lightweight, built by E. G. Young, Nottingham.

This is possibly the only picture of a machine of 1908. Courtesy of TCM

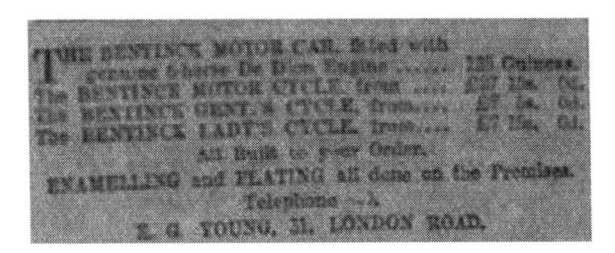

The Bentinck Car fitted with 6hp De Dion Engine. BNA.

Mr Young remained at London Rd to about 1912, then moved to larger premises at Arkwright Street, Nottingham, to concentrate on car production. By then E.W. Young and Company had become the Bentinck Motor Company after the late Lord Henry Bentinck.

In this Chapter I also wanted to include another lesser-known manufacturer of a Nottingham motorcycle.

An Engine with Overhead Valves, Camshafts, and Other Unique Features.

Built by Mr R.G. Baird of Nottingham, this powerful 750cc machine was completely built at home. The engine, similar to a car with a horizontally split crankcase had hand turned pistons with two rings and was a shaft drive. The rear suspension is a unique design that apparently worked well. Sadly, she never went into production, and Mr Baird was declared bankrupt trying. What a shame no one helped?
Thanks to TCM Publications for providing the above.

CAMPION INNOVATION.

Here are a number of interesting details that are listed in date order.
1911. All chain drive available and a separate oil tank.

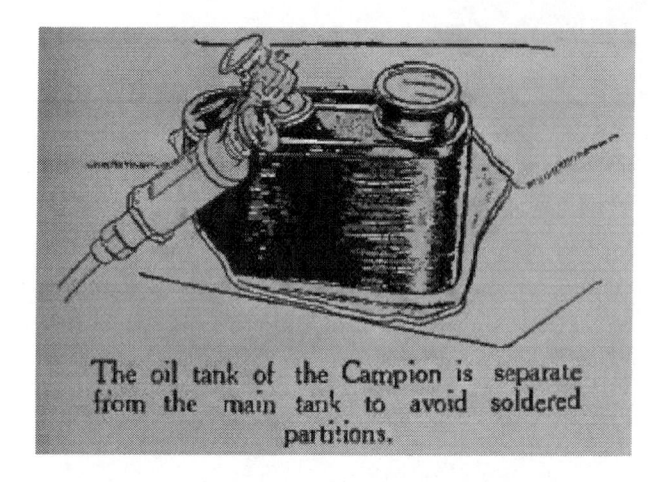

The oil tank of the Campion is separate from the main tank to avoid soldered partitions.

Due to vibration the soldered joint separating the oils used to leak, contaminating the fuel. This was a simple solution that could be fitted to the existing tank, or on the seat down tube.

G. F. Campion and the wireless telegraphy apparatus attached to his motor cycle.

George Campion in 1911 came up with the idea of being able to transmit and receive radio messages whilst mobile. This worked well of speeds up to 30mph depending on the length of the Ariel and contact to earth., This proved successful. The initial idea was for use cycle meetings but was also for military use.

The receiving apparatus.

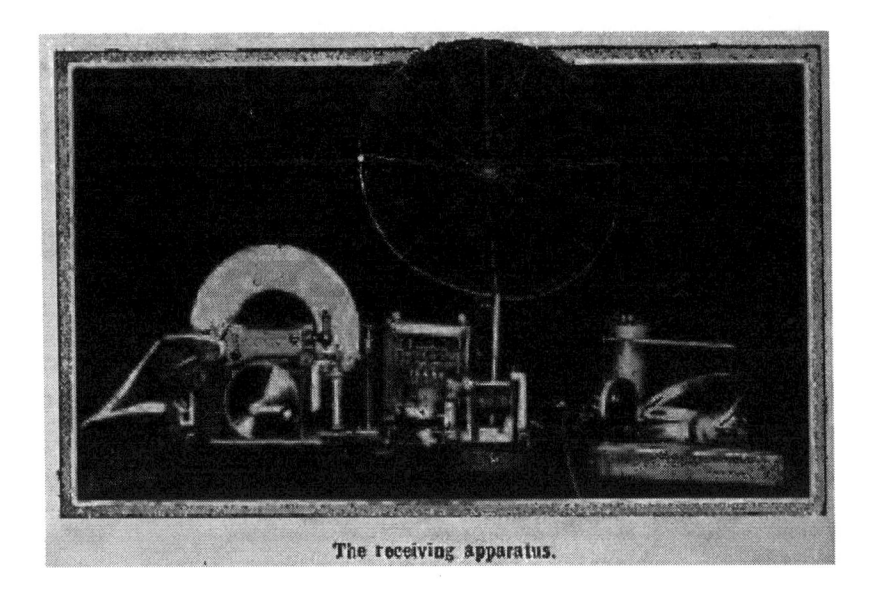

Please do not drop or leave out in the rain?

Campion was also credited with the easily removable rear mudguard giving easy access to rear wheel for punctures and removal, see Chapter relating to Models.

1914.

The Jardine 4 speed gearbox, was used initially for competition on the larger machines and sidecars, but not coming into production till 1915 where it became fitted to larger machines until 1922. A Jardine 2 and 3 speed box was also fitted on smaller machines.

The balloon was an experimentation of fuels during the war. Lots of time was spent on this development. You remember the same fitted to the Dads Army Jones butchers van. See Wartime Chapter. Campion also supplied kits of the above. Here is George again, and family in 1916. Accreditation to Nottingham City Council and Picture the Past Organisation.

A rear-sprung hub was used. No details are available at present. It was subsequently discontinued. I will continue to search?

1917.

First use of the ambulance sidecars patented the year after, with sidecars taking two persons, (See Wartime Chapter and Sidecar Chapter).

Also an all aluminium lightweight sports sidecar was built but again patented 1919.

1920.

Credited for the first Sidecar Taxi (see Sidecar Chapter).

1921.

Fully enclosed chain case on sidecars and taxis. Oil fed from crankcase.
About this year the 10hp Blackburne powered machine was evolved, and used with great success in competition.

1922.

Enclosed expanding brakes on sidecars first at the rear of the motorcycle then on both wheels. These wheels were interchangeable. An expanding brake was added later to the sidecar.

1923.

Aero Forks, developed by Campion from 1921, fitted to the larger machines. Were not patented to 1923 and 1924. The fork design appears to have continued for a year or so later going back to the trusted Druids but still with the latest Druid top sprung linkage. Bamford Forks were also used.

I have noticed a heavily braced lower linkage on competition and taxis.
Please see Chapter relating to Models.

I have also enclosed a couple of interesting private enterprise ideas, which are worth a mention. The first is rear springing on a Campion, the second is running a two stroke on diesel?

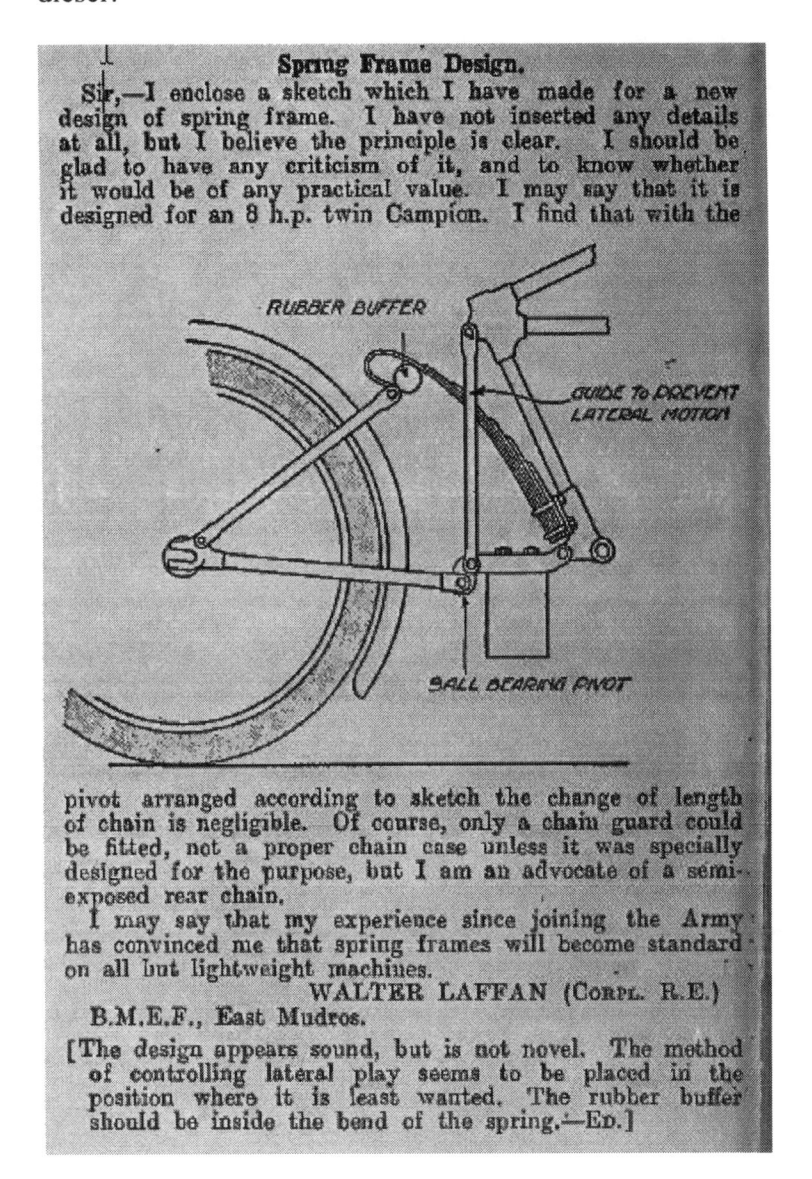

Spring Frame Design.

Sir,—I enclose a sketch which I have made for a new design of spring frame. I have not inserted any details at all, but I believe the principle is clear. I should be glad to have any criticism of it, and to know whether it would be of any practical value. I may say that it is designed for an 8 h.p. twin Campion. I find that with the pivot arranged according to sketch the change of length of chain is negligible. Of course, only a chain guard could be fitted, not a proper chain case unless it was specially designed for the purpose, but I am an advocate of a semi-exposed rear chain.

I may say that my experience since joining the Army has convinced me that spring frames will become standard on all but lightweight machines.

WALTER LAFFAN (Corpl. R.E.)
B.M.E.F., East Mudros.

[The design appears sound, but is not novel. The method of controlling lateral play seems to be placed in the position where it is least wanted. The rubber buffer should be inside the bend of the spring.—Ed.]

> There were a few ideas around but what a good idea for the period? There would be lateral movement where the buffer is indicated, but that could be sorted, even with a damper?

2 ¾ hp Villiers Campion, with the owner's own solid wheels, and fuel modification.

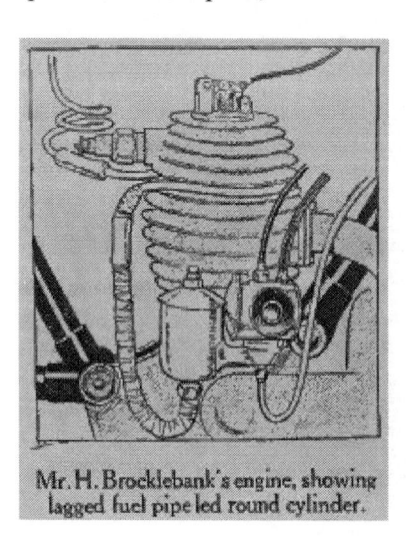

Mr. H. Brocklebank's engine, showing lagged fuel pipe led round cylinder.

The Campion above could run on paraffin or diesel. The float chamber being bent around the cylinder to be as close to heat as possible. The fuel line being bent around the fins of the barrel then lagged to the float chamber.
There was a sighted drip feed for lubrication also fitted. Would hate to be riding behind him?

I have found many examples of advertising, but here are three more examples.

This is a Campion Light Up aid, which popped in the tax disc holder. Thanks to Mr Jackson for this. They were popular till after WW2 with other marques.

This is a pencil, given away at local depots. This one is from the Lincoln Cycle Co, Corporation Street, Lincoln. If you keep your eyes open, this type of advertising can still be found and wonderful to collect?

This photograph of a tram at Derby, about 1900 is a great example of Campion advertising on local transport. I have seen them on trams in Nottingham and Surrounding Counties. They had a depot on London Road, Derby for many years.

Another factor I came across whilst compiling this was the number of places Campion found themselves around the world. This was their export list.

France, Germany, Austria, Spain, Portugal, Denmark, Finland, Holland, Italy, South America, Cape Colony, Natal, Transvaal, The Orange Free State, Rhodesia, Egypt, Australia, India, China, Burma, and Singapore. Better check my passport?

Further advertising? This picture is on the famous Bunny Hill. Dated 1911, Charles is in control. In the sidecar, the rear passenger is George Hunt. In front is Alfred. Not sure of the pillion. This machine had chain drive, and forward pegs.

To finish this Chapter it has to be George Campion, dated 1907. His contribution to the company was tireless. He was also a keen archaeologist in Nottingham. Thank you to Mr Holdsworth and Picture the Past for the use of this photograph.

CAMPION AND HENRY CURRY

Henry Curry originally founded the Company in Leicester in 1884. He began working for the Leicester Tricycle Company where he learned his trade and then from home produced early bicycles similar to Campion. These were distributed through local shops, the first opening in Leicester in 1888 at 271 Belgrave Gate. The business was known as H. Curry and Sons from 1897. Henry's sons, James, Edwin, Albert and Henry, joined their father in the business, which then retailed toys and later wirelesses up to 1927.

Whether Henry had met Edwin or William at some point via trade shows we will never know, but certainly at the Leicester Show of 1911, the suggestion they had met is made as they were displaying motorcycles together. May be this is just wishful thinking, as the report covers the two companies that infer this, however there was a branch of Curry's in Nottingham at this time, so may be? It is also possible that Campion instigated the Curry motorcycle, but we will never know? There is more detail of the Curry's Motorcycle in the chapter relating to Models. Little if anything is known about this. 1913 has been suggested as a date for a Curry's machine but again no details are available. Henry Curry had retired in 1910 so if this is accurate, it leaves his sons responsible for this?

The machine was not produced in considerable numbers, as I can find no further contributions to the motorcycle industry from this firm, other than the formation of The Swadlincote M.C.C. at a Curry's Cycle Depot in 1911. In fact there is very little information available of the earlier years of the company, even by way of advertising. I can trace no sales of second hand machinery either, but that does not mean there are none left?

One can take it that the motorcycle was not a success, hence the trail dries up, but what attracted Curry's to the Campion Cycle Company in the first place? The story goes that they took Campion over in 1927, primarily for the retail outlets and the facilities of hire purchase. Financing cycles then motorcycles and cars, was something Campion had been involved with since the last century. Having been fortunate to read the original documents of the take over, there was a lot more to it.

I have mentioned before that Mr E. Hutchinson took a serious participating role within Campion's. It is he that connects with the Curry's board of Directors, namely James, Edwin and Henry. There is no mention of Edwin or the other members of the family. One such meeting of the directors was described as an extraordinary meeting, and from that one can conclude that all in Campion household were not happy?

Curry's suggestion was to amalgamate the two companies by way of moving both to Leicester under the Curry's name. That did not happen. Searches of Campion's accounts relating to all the leases of the outlets complicated the period of the take over. The Robin Hood Street factory was valued, and so was the Leicester factory. Machinery and stock likewise. It was clear that new premises were to be looked for at Leicester then Birmingham and Coventry. Halfords were approached as a purchase, then the Mead Cycle Company at Birmingham, who again refused a deal with Curry's. In the mean time, Curry's acquired Campion's shares, and let them continue limited production whilst a solution could be found. That control was enough to strangle the company. All concerned would loose money. In 1927 the Directors were in effect, paid off, and instructed to resign at the end of the year. Mr Hutchinson was kept on to oversee the take over and current sales.

> operations on the limited scale in force since the control passed to Messrs. Currys (1927) Limited, have been justified. As against

In the meantime existing parts, machinery and stock were put together and sold through the depots. Blackburne engines were still being delivered and used in machines. H. Curry and Sons 1927 chose at this time to go Limited.

> STOCK IN TRADE. £29,702. 14. 11. The stock in trade is analysed as follows:-
> Retail Branches.
>   Accessories.   £4,792. 18. 7.
>   Motor Cycles and Motor
>   Cars.   9,230. 6. 11.
>   Electric Goods.   182. 18. 2.
>   Gramophones and Records.   1,003. 9. 6.
>   Toys.   874. 2. 4.
>   Wireless Goods.   750. 11. 2.
>   Cycles.   2,690. 9. 3.
>   Frame and Side Lines.   769. 16. 4.
>   20,294. 12. 3.
> Nottingham Factory.
>   Materials and Stores.   6,783. 6. 9.
>   Finished Cycles.   2,624. 15. 11.
>   9,408. 2. 8.
>   £29,702. 14. 11.

The Liverpool Street factory was sold for about £11000. By 1929, Curry's still had not sold their factory, but had been instructed to complete the deal by the beginning of 1930. There was an eternal time lapse of accounts, verifications, re valuation, sales, and on going costs etc. Unfortunately Mr Hutchinson died in 1929, and by 1930 Edwin Campion had set up as E.W. Campion and Sons on Bathley Street, also Station Street Nottingham, and was already at Grantham. George Campion set up producing his own cycles.

The Mead Cycle Company had now gone into liquidation, and acquired by Curry's, so they at last had a new location to move to. The deal was now a very protracted and a messy one. The Campion Carlton Depot in 1930 was now retailing Campion cycles, Curry Cycles, Hercules Cycles and radios. There was no mention of Campion motorcycles. Obviously, these were now end of lines. Some branches, were kept on under the Curry's (1927) Ltd, others were closed. Members of the Campion factory found work at Mr Hutchinson Textiles, and Edwin Campion new depots. Curry's did not get possession of new premises at Birmingham till 1931. Curry's factory at Leicester did not sell till 1932, so the initial proposal could not have physically happened, instead Campion had been asset stripped and turned into a financial house. It took three years from acquiring the shares to completion? The change of name did not go down well with the Campion Directors either. Curry's ceased to produce any more cycles. Instead they used the Curry's name on Hercules machines, but gained the 20 financial outlets required. They continued to import electrical products and the rest is history!

It makes me wonder what would have happened to both companies if the deal had not gone through at all, never mind over three years? Maybe Campion would have gone bankrupt, who knows? It does show, even in those times, that organisation was not at its best, and the deal sadly lacked planning.

One thing I will mention, call me a romantic, but I believe there was a little guilt left with the Curry brothers. Below is a picture of a late Curry's cycle. You can see the Curry's logo as was, within the large letter C. I would like to think that this was done to relate to Campion. May be not, but why have it designed as such? I leave you with that thought?

CAMPION FINALLY?

Campion name continued in the motor trade till the 1980's. The name was seen on original buildings but the Campion Marque had long gone. During their time they made an impact in the textile, bicycle, and motorcycle industry. They also contributed considerably to Nottingham employment and economy. During their peak they were producing some 400 bicycles and up to 45 motorcycles a week. Here, they are remembered.

I hope you have enjoyed this presentation of the Campion family and their success in Industry in Nottingham. I have uncovered considerable information, however I cannot include it all. There are more photos and advertisements. Some are in bad shape and so the best and more relevant you see here. I hope more details come to light, then may be we can cover another publication? I am also still searching for another machine, whether bicycle or motorcycle to restore? Who knows?

The only question remaining is, Are you a Campionite?

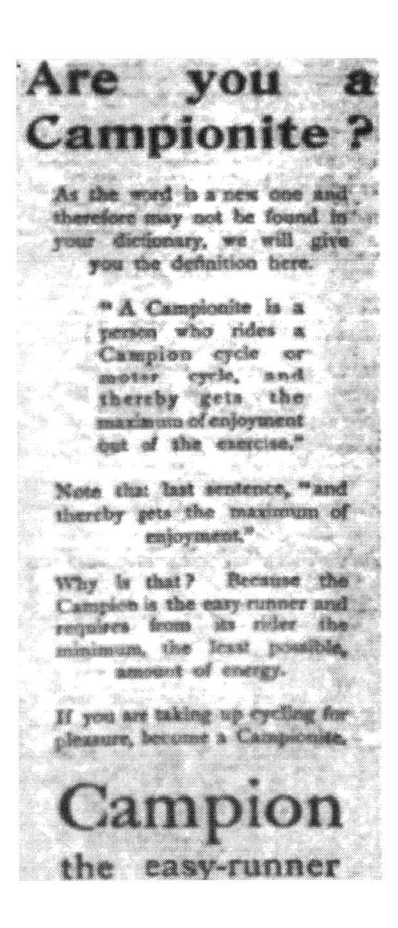

BIBOLOGRAPHY

The below mentioned publications have been used for reference, although two have little detail. A considerable amount of information has come from many other sources with genuine period documents that have been kindly loaned, given, or purchased to produce this book.

The British Archives.
The British Newspaper Archives.
The British Patent Office.
The Curry Group Plc Archives.
The Encyclopaedia of the Motorcycle by Peter Henshaw.
The Evening Post.
Grace's Guide.
The Illustrated Encyclopaedia of Motorcycles by Erwin Tragatsch.
The Light Car by C.F. Caunter.
The London Gazette.
Motor Marine & Aircraft Red Book, 1913-1917.
Motor Sport Magazine Archives.
The Motor Cycle.
Made in Nottingham by Brian Waters and Richard English.
Oldbike. The Online Bicycle Museum.
The Register of Machines by William Hume
The Thomas Humber Story.
The Thoroton Society of Nottingham.
The Veteran and Vintage Motorcycle Club.

PICTURE CREDITS

The following people have contributed pictures presented in this book. Without them it simply would not have been possible.

Alistair Brown who provided photos of his 1921 Campion.

John Beaty who provided a great number of genuine photographs and documentation. They gave me an incite into the company and the enthusiasm to record it.

The British Newspaper Archives. Newspaper images (C) The British Library Board. All Rights Preserved. They provide a great service to research. Try and use them?

Mike Caldwell, known for his Rover Links, who kindly gave me a fascinating afternoon photographing his Bicycles. Thank you.

Phillip Jackson who not only provided photos of his 4hp but also his two cycles.

Len Kelly for his picture of his machine in Australia.

Colin Kirsch who contributed early information.

Waldema Osinski for his photos of the 1912 sidecar outfit.

Tony Phelps for contributions re Albert Ball.

Joe Rush again provided pictures of his early Campion /Precision, that when he purchased her, was sat on a sideboard. A suitable and fitting location!

Picture the Past, who linked with different counties, collect and preserve photographs that otherwise, would be lost. They have provided many great quality period photos as indicated.

TCM Publications. Where would we be if publishers did not retain or purchase historical documents and photographs? They provided many press cuttings and period reports.

John Williams for the pictures of Albert Ball.

ACKNOWLEDGEMENTS

I have covered many above, thank you again. Others also helped.
To begin with Keith Wakling from the VMCC, who without his help guidance and loan of patterns, I would not have finished my machine or learned of information thus recorded. We often conversed over recording what we know? So I suppose it is his entire fault I wrote this? Thanks mate.

John Beaty who's original Campion photographs documentation, and general wonderful disposition was enough to inspire me to really get this thing moving.

Alan Beet, my friend who transported me to all ports of call at a moment's notice and above all is a fellow enthusiast.

Brian Binns who is a relative through marriage to William Campion. Brian provided lots of family details, which was enough to confuse any one. He provided other research and documentation, which I am grateful for. His enthusiasm is none comparable with any one I have ever met. I hope the result is a fitting tribute to a great family?

Angie Emery, not just for the coffee but importantly her support to finish the project.

Richard English for linked information and support.

The Nottingham Industrial Museum and Archives for advice and contributions.

Peter Rodgers who at a moments notice sorted out my lap top, programmes, and when I lost the first edition and back ups, retrieved the lap top from the bin and pointed me in the right direction, again?

The Tyre guys at Beaulieu, for providing details on models, wheel and tyre sizes. Thereby sorting my own machine.

The Veteran Cycle Club for the use of the library and numerous conversations. A great bunch of enthusiasts who have really nailed it down with preservation.

The Veteran and Vintage Motorcycle Club for archive access and guidance, in particular the library chaps and Rob Reany.

Finally, Bill and Doris Crofts. Nottingham people who were keen motorcyclists and in the 1950's bought their new BSA 650 A10 from Campion on Station Street. As well as being my parents they were ultimately responsible for my keen interest in motorcycles. Dad died in 95, followed by mum this year (2016). They would enjoy this! X

DERBYSHIRE
& Co
CAMPION DEPOT
SPIRIT & OILS
CAMPION MOTORS
CAMPION CYCLES
CAMPION
CAMPION
the easy=runner